To David + Eve
with love
Ro S.u.

GW00703442

AFRICAN DAYS

AFRICAN DAYS

Memories of Southern Rhodesia, 1956–57

Robin Dean

Book Guild Publishing
Sussex, England

First published in Great Britain in 2012 by
The Book Guild Ltd
Pavilion View
19 New Road
Brighton, BN1 1UF

Typesetting in Garamond by
Ellipsis Digital Limited, Glasgow

Printed and bound in Great Britain by
CPI Group (UK) Ltd, Croydon, CR0 4YY

A catalogue record for this book is available from The British Library.

ISBN 978 1 84624 757 6

In memory of my parents who made this African adventure possible for me. Especially to my mother who kept all of my African letters intact. I discovered them after her death, tucked away in a drawer of her bureau desk.

To Jean Mumford for her patience in deciphering these old faded airmail letters in order to type up this manuscript.

Introduction

As I look out of my window over the lovely rolling hills of Galloway, this view reminds me in many ways of those heather clad hills of Inyanga which happened to be my home some fifty six years ago when I first set foot on what was then Southern Rhodesia, an adventure which made such a lasting impression on me.

It all started through the fact that my father served in North Africa during the 'Desert Campaign' and aftermath as Camp Commandant for the Canal Zone. It was through him and his friend Major General 'Ricky' Richards, both of whom made many friends with those Rhodesians and South Africans who came up to serve with their respective Armoured Brigades during the North African Campaign, that I had so many names of those who fought alongside the British Army. And after the war ended, these very generous friends would send us not only Christmas cards, but also very much welcomed food parcels made up mostly of tinned and dried South African fruit. Along with the Christmas cards would be requests for my parents to travel out to South Africa. However, my father being by then committed to his farming and business enterprises wrote in reply that he had a son of a certain age who had a desire to travel.

That was how I started my adventure. Born in the early 1930s, I was the product of that lucky generation as I was too young to have served in the Second World War unlike my father, who happened to have served in both world wars. Fortunately he survived the horrors of the First World War, to be called upon again in 1939 at the outbreak of the Second World War, having served with the T.A. during the inter-war years. His first appointment was an attachment to what was then known as Southern Command being stationed

1

on the south coast awaiting the imminent invasion which fortunately never happened. After what was then known as the "phoney war" the invasion threat died away and he was then posted to North Africa. My mother meanwhile ran our family property near a little town called Usk situated in the beautiful Usk valley in the county of Monmouthshire.

My mother was a remarkably resourceful woman in so many ways having been brought up in Southern Ireland from an Anglo Irish background known as the 'Ascendancy'. As a young girl she witnessed the burning of her family home by the Sinn Fein, 'Derrylahan Park', which was situated halfway between the town of Birr Co Offaly and Portumna on the river Shannon.

After the loss of Derrylahan my grandparents came and settled in Shropshire where my mother met and married my father and started her married life in Monmouthshire.

It fell upon her shoulders at the outbreak of the war to run, not only our lovely home Glen Usk, but also the family farm, as well as working for the Red Cross and other war charities. One of the charitable endeavours was to make our home a place of rest and recreation for young Commonwealth pilots, who in many cases had no immediate families to go to during their rest periods from flying operations over Europe.

Of the many young pilots who stayed with us, one particular young officer from the Royal Australian Air force became a special friend of ours. His name was Bill Chase and he came from a Queensland farming background. We all had fond memories of him, and it was so inspiring to think that he was not much older than both my brother and me, flying Lancaster bombers over Europe; he was very much a hero in our young eyes.

I still remember the night when he had my brother and me lying on our backs on the front lawn, Bill explaining to us the stars and how he would use them to navigate his aircraft across Europe on bombing missions. It was not long after that occasion when my poor mother received that dreaded telegram announcing that Bill had been reported missing over northern Europe. It was only sometime afterwards we all learnt that he went down with his aircraft. For the rest of her life my mother wore the R.A.A.F. (Royal Australian Air Force) brooch which Bill gave her, in his memory.

After the war my mother I believe met Bill's mother who ran the family sheep station. She also became my sister Victoria's godmother, as well as calling her Queensland property after our home 'Glen Usk' in memory of Bill's last happy days with us.

I myself was packed off to my prep school in 1942, a school called Mostyn House situated in the Wirral of Cheshire. I can't quite remember why I started at the early age of seven, however, it could have been that I had two cousins at that school. I started the long train journey from south Wales to Chester with instructions that I had to give up my seat to a serviceman, so most of my journey was spent in the coach corridor which suited me as I was by then an avid 'train spotter'. These north to south trains were always packed, mostly with naval ratings travelling between Portsmouth, Plymouth, Rosyth and further north to Scapa Flow, many of whom, like me, preferred the corridors so that they could easily mingle with their mates and also smoke.

I cannot say that I had fond memories of my time at Mostyn House as, by then, the war had put so many restrictions on, especially regarding food. I particularly disliked tapioca puddings and boiled cabbage in which one had to pick out cooked caterpillars of the cabbage white butterflies. But I do remember the air raids when both Birkenhead and Liverpool were targeted by the German Luftwaffe, the red glow to the north as we emerged out of our air raid shelter indicating the devastating effect of the bombing on those two cities. Also an occasional stray bomb would land nearby, shaking our shelter.

My time at Mostyn House was punctuated by a spell in hospital, as I had contracted osteomyelitis, an inflammation of my left leg which had to be operated on by a Polish Jewish refugee surgeon. I must say I owe to him the saving of my leg, as it was he who recognised the disease of the bone marrow as a form of TB. My convalescence on crutches, which eventually got me back on two legs took six months.

I always eagerly awaited my holidays going home to Glen Usk. My mother would lovingly greet me off the train at Pontypool station because she, with her meagre allowance of petrol which she was allocated as a bona fide farmer, managed to use the car for such occasions.

My holidays were always enlightened by the entourage of young pilots, various cousins and, after 1943, American servicemen who had set up a base nearby, in order to practise bridge building across the river Usk. We all hoped that this bridge would be a permanent structure but sadly it was not to be, as it was all dismantled for shipment to Europe after the D Day landings.

However, the Americans were more than welcome with their nylons, candy and so many unheard of luxuries, and were greeted with open arms. My brother Martin and I hoarded candy hidden around the house like squirrels, and I believe we made ourselves ill with over-indulgence.

With all the coming and goings of U.S. military personnel my brother and I became fascinated by the Jeeps and it was not long before we were offered a ride in one by a kindly officer who on visiting my mother, instructed his driver to take the two boys for a spin. We were whisked through the countryside in an open Jeep much to our excitement.

Another factor which brought new faces into our lives was, firstly, the land girls, who helped on our farm, shortly followed by Italian prisoners of war. These were something of a mixed blessing with my mother and the then farm manager due to having to intervene, along with the local camp commandant to prevent fights amongst the Italians, mostly due to the pretty housemaid we employed at the time. The housemaid was put in the family way, much to the interest of our local village who were then more looking forward to the birth of a little 'bambino' than my mother's impending birth of my sister Victoria!

After a while the Italians were all repatriated except for one who was allowed to stay on in Britain as he had married a local girl.

The Italians were followed by Germans, who in many ways were model prisoners, hard working, especially one who happened to be a very good mechanic in keeping our aged farm machinery going. But as the war ended a number of these Germans who had come from what was to be East Germany to be then occupied by the Russians, did their utmost to stay on in Britain. Sadly they were all sent back to Germany and we never knew what happened to those who ended up in the East Zone. With the declaration of peace, May 1945, I was summoned with all our school to await the announcement from the headmaster that the European war had ended. There was a great cheer from us all, boys and staff alike. But everyone knew there was to be a long hard road ahead for the country. V. E. Day was soon followed by a Labour victory. My mother was somewhat put out that her faithful daily help had voted 'Labour' and on being confronted she replied of course Winston Churchill will join the 'Labour Party'. Shades of when Winston left the Liberals for the Conservatives.

My recollections of those early post war years was if you wanted anything you had to get it through the black market and the word 'spiv' became part of our culture.

As Britain struggled to regain strength in the economy the country was beset with one of the worst winters in decades in 1947. This almost brought the nation to its knees, through shortages of coal and the distribution of basic food stuffs. This long winter lasted right through to April with snow drifts still lying in country lanes until May.

The only added joy to us was that my father had been demobbed, and was now running the farm. During the worst of the snow falls he would equip himself with his skis in order to travel across country inspecting the livestock, and the only way we could fodder them was to make up a sledge to be pulled by one of our ponies, taking out hay and also water as everything had frozen up with no running water to the drinking troughs.

On leaving my prep school I went on to follow my Posnett cousins to Stowe which was very much to my liking with the wonderful freedom to roam the beautiful Bridgeman gardens, the wealth of temples by Vanbrugh, Gibbs and William Kent, all of which made a lasting impression on me with my love of architecture. And now having the pleasure of today seeing this beautiful landscape restored along with Stowe House – a joy forever.

I was very fortunate in that my early years at Stowe coincided with the final year of J. F. Roxburgh, the founding headmaster. Also, at that time many of the younger masters had been away on war service. J.F., as he was known, recruited some of his contemporaries from his university days, all of whom were born in the nineteenth century and held good Edwardian and Victorian values. I was blessed in sharing their wisdom and experiences, and they taught me how to enjoy the good things in life; art, literature and classical music.

On leaving Stowe it seemed that all my generation of school leavers had a career to enter into, with most following their father's profession or business. I was designated to be a farmer, which was of course my father's wish. So I went on to the Royal Agricultural College, Cirencester. Meanwhile, prior to joining my chosen course 'Estate Management' I was sent away to be a 'Mud Student' on the Cally Estate in Kirkcudbrightshire under the watchful eye of Betty Murray Usher, who was then a noted breeder of the famous 'Galloway' beef cattle. I have happy recollections of my time doing all sorts of tasks from 'tattie picking' along with hosts of school children which was the norm of those days, taking charge of a milking herd of Ayrshire cows, lambing up in the hills which meant living in a caravan, those lovely Scottish dawns with the sun rising over the hills, the calls of curlews, lapwings and grouse. Trying not to step on adders who came out to bask in the early sunrise, one felt very close to nature.

However, those same hills are now silent owing to afforestation with a blanket cover of Sitka spruce resulting in a dramatic change in what was lovely heather moorland.

As fate would have it Betty Murray Usher was my late wife's godmother. We both had such fond memories of our times with 'Emu', as she was known. Jan herself was from a Galloway family, the Landales of Dalswinton, so on my retirement we both decided to return to live in that lovely unspoilt part of south west Scotland.

Looking back, my two years at the Royal Agricultural College were my happiest, especially as being a young adult in the early 1950s was for me very exciting. Britain was at long last finding its feet again and one felt the word 'Great' had finally been joined up with Britain.

The country seemed then to lead the world with so many achievements, notably the 1951 Festival of Britain followed by the Coronation of Queen Elizabeth II in 1953 heralding the new era of hope and promises. I remember so well on the morning of the Coronation being greeted by a Thames waterman on landing at the Westminster Pier with the news that Everest had been conquered. The reason why we had landed that morning was the fact that my father had secured a mooring for his yacht opposite the Palace of Westminster.

I believe the re-election of a Conservative administration led again by Winston Churchill quickened the pace of recovery. Rationing became just a memory, there was a new dawn of air travel as Britain led the world in the introduction of innovatory jet aircraft such as the Comet (sadly after an unfortunate start with two crashes). The Britannia and the Viscount meant smooth comfortable travel worldwide.

Our motor industry at that period was booming. We were then the second largest manufacturers of motor vehicles after America. But I do remember reading a report written by a delegation of our motor manufacturers who travelled to Japan to survey the embryonic Japanese motor industry. Their report ended with the quote that the Japanese cars will be of no consequence or threat to our own motor industry, but their motor cycles could cause problems for our manufacturers. How wrong was the former statement, how right was the second prediction.

During the 1950s what was so exciting to a young motoring enthusiast like myself was the resounding successes of our Jaguar and Aston Martin sports racing at such prestigious events as the

Le Mans 24 hour race held every year in June. Nearer home the racing circuit at Silverstone became a big draw as I started to visit this circuit when I was at Stowe which happened to be just a few miles away. I had the honour to attend the first Grand Prix to be held post war in 1948. The 1950s also held such happy memories for my generation, with wonderful musical shows such as Salad Days, My Fair Lady, South Pacific and West Side Story. There were many others including films which featured Alec Guinness, Margaret Rutherford and Alistair Sim, as well as Stanley Holloway in the show 'The Crazy Gang'. Also The Windmill Theatre was a great draw to all of us who were young at that time. The London Debutante season was by then in full swing. Dancing to the likes of Edmundo Ros and Pilbeam's bands, the memories all bring such happy times back to me. In many ways what my parents enjoyed in the 1920s was repeated for my generation in the 1950s.

After leaving Cirencester with encouragement from my parents, I duly set sail for South Africa with my journey starting at the Pool of London when I joined my ship, the M.V. *City of York*. She was one of the Ellerman Line vessels on the South African run, a voyage of seventeen days to Capetown with one stop at Las Palmas, Gran Canaria. Unlike the Union Castle ships, the M.V. *City of York* had only about thirty passengers. By the time we disembarked everybody had got to know each other. Most of the passengers were South Africans, a small number such as myself were travelling out for the first time. One such family were emigrating to start a new life in Northern Rhodesia with a complete engineering factory on board packed away in the hold of the ship.

On the long sea voyage, in addition to shipboard party games, there was ample opportunity to read up some historical background to both South Africa and of course the two Rhodesias. I was recommended firstly the book *Matabele Thompson* written and published by his daughter Nancy Rouillard which covered the early endeavours by Cecil Rhodes, his lifelong associates Charles Dunell Rudd and Francis Robert Thompson, who obtained a concession for mining from Lobengula the king of Matebele granted in 1888, which was to be the political foundation of Southern Rhodesia.

Two other books I chose were, *Trekking On* by Denys Reitz, written prior to the Boer war and its aftermath and Laurens van der Post's *Venture to the Interior*, his travels through Nyasaland and beyond. Visiting Mt. Mulanje captured my imagination about what was in store for me on my arrival in Southern Rhodesia.

On arrival at Capetown I was greeted by my friend Douglas Leighton Seager who was a more than generous host in showing me around the city and its environs. What struck me was a visit to the shanty towns all of which had sprung up in what is now known as the Cape flats on the outskirts of Capetown. They catered for a mixed race, part African and European who had the misfortune to be designated by the South African Nationalist government of the day, 'a race known as coloureds', falling outside both African and European but historically through relationships between the two races over two hundred years.

With my young and rather liberal upbringing I was very conscious of the rules and regulations of what was known as apartheid. All public transport was segregated; whites rode up front of both trains and buses but woe betide you if you should cross the divide. I was also aware there were starting to be freedom movements such as the 'Black Sash' headed by a very brave Helen Suzman, incidentally the mother of the actress Janet Suzman, who stood silently outside public buildings especially the parliament house in Capetown itself in protest against the Nationalist government and apartheid by wearing black sashes. I witnessed this sight for myself along with what my friends explained to me was the more liberal Cape Province English-speaking police being quietly replaced by hard line Afrikaners from the Free State. The noose was slowly tightening on the more liberal English speaking Cape and its culture.

After a stay of more than ten days I duly boarded my train with all my luggage for a four day journey north to Salisbury travelling via De Aar, Kimberley, Mafeking crossing over into Bechuanaland then into Southern Rhodesia. I changed trains at Bulawayo onto a very smart clean train with coaches painted in the style of the old Great Western chocolate and cream of the Rhodesian Railways to my final destination Salisbury, to be met at the Meikles Hotel by Hilary Wryley Birch. My African Days had begun.

Qwaraguzi
Inyanga
S. Rhodesia

June 8th 1956

Dear Mummy

Thank you very much for your last letter. I was sorry to hear about Mr Kimmins' [our gardener at Glenusk] death. I never expected him to die as I rather regarded that he would live for many years yet, especially since he moved to Court Perrot.

I am very pleased about Stella's prize I hope we can get her back when she has returned from hunt racing.

I stayed in Salisbury for a few days before the Wyrley Birches met me and it gave me a chance to explore the city. It is a very attractive city laid out beautifully with gardens and parks. The streets are so wide that I found it a risky business crossing them and had to run for it on several occasions. I spent my time looking after a Dutchman who I met on the train. He is also going to farm. The shops are very good and there are new buildings going up in all directions all of the skyscraper pattern.

Mrs Wyrley Birch came to meet me; she is just like what General Richards described her to me. A Mrs Russell Clark but more untidy. She is almost a split image tall and thin. When I met her at my hotel she had seven girls from her daughter's school in the car, we all went out to spend the day at a friend's house in the suburbs. This friend of hers had seven children which is quite normal for Rhodesia and the elder are married so when lunch came there were 25 people and some more dropped in during the afternoon and tea came round it had gone up to 30! Which

I gather is not unusual in this country. It is easy with the black servants.

Mrs W. Birch had to go in hospital for a massage to her back, so I went to Inyanga by train and bus as she couldn't leave for a few days. I must say the Rhodesian trains are excellent compared with the British and the service is good and cheap; most trains are diesel powered so they are beautifully clean. At a place called Rusapi I disembarked and boarded the Inyanga bus for another 60 miles. I had great fun on boarding, as lots of little black boys rushed forward to take my luggage and they started a free fight amongst themselves to who should take what. I am amazed how my luggage stayed together and no handles taken off the suitcases.

The bus journey was amusing as we travelled in the front compartment whilst the rear was full of Africans who piled on the top of the bus with all their luggage such as bicycles, suitcases and various bundles. Along the road the bus would lurch into one of the many pot holes and everything would come tumbling off the top, chickens in cages, bicycles the lot would be strewn all over the road.

I was almost in hysterics as they would replace everything on the top their excitement was so great that it would fall down the other side whenever they tried to put it in position. Along the route the bus would stop and we all alighted and had cups of tea at various farmsteads which is typical of Rhodesian hospitality.

It was quite dark when I got to the Rhodes hotel where I was to meet Col Wyrley Birch just before it got dark I managed to get a good glimpse of the country which is quite beautiful, lovely mountains and hills just like Scotland.

Col Wyrley Birch met me in an old Ford V8 like ours except it was a post war model and we went charging off up to Qwaraguzi. On the way up we stopped at a spot where a lion had been spotted the night before and the Col had a rifle at the ready in the car in case of an encounter but we saw nothing. The roads here are quite unbelievably bad and only the old American cars or a Land Rover last at all. The English cars just break up. The Wyrley Birches also have a Chevrolet.

Qwaraguzi is a lovely house in a most unusual style which is typical Rhodesian: each wing is a separate block and one has to walk outside to get from the dining room to the sitting room. I have a separate little cottage on the end. Everybody in Africa gets up with the sun and goes to bed with the sun. So we start our day at 7 am. The mornings are quite beautiful with a slight frost and the rolling mists among the hills. The days are not hot, as it is the winter. The sun gets warm if there is no cloud and the temperature goes up to 70 degrees.

The whole district is settled by ex army officers, colonels and majors are very much in evidence. I have had the chance to meet some of them already and they are all typically British Army. I have also met two Hanmer brothers who have farms adjoining here. The W. Birches have a married son who lives down in the village of Inyanga some ten miles from here. He runs their butchers shop and mills which is a very successful enterprise. Most of the Europeans are gradually giving up farming and turning their attentions to commercial undertakings as the Africans are beginning to come into their own in the farming world.

This is a wonderful house as there are at least 10 dogs including 5 hound puppies and also 4 cats live under the same roof. In my bedroom I have a family of lizards which run over the walls keeping the flies down. They are very amusing to watch.

I have been doing some riding as horses are the best means of cross country transport here. We visit various dipping centres as the cattle have to be dipped at least once a week because of the ticks. Leopards and hyenas take a terrible toll of cows, calves and sheep and we are endlessly setting traps. The African hunting boys are excellent at this.

The W. Birches are extraordinary nice and very generous and I have the use of their cars at any time I wish.

Douglas L. Seager is coming up next weekend to see me.

Lots of love
From Robin

Qwaraguzi
Inyanga
S. Rhodesia

June 14th 1956

Dear Mummy

Thank you very much for the letter concerning the Bath and West. We seemed to have quite a satisfactory result.

I am having a most enjoyable time here, and during the last week I have been staying down with Col Wyrley Birch's son Anthony who runs the butchery and dairy. I have been managing the farm for him. During the week I bought 10 pigs at £10 each. They are breeding sows and one boar. I had to collect them from a farm some 16 miles from here. I borrowed the Native Commissionaire's lorry with a native driver. The lorry was an old Bedford and it had a leaking radiator, and I had to stop it by putting mealie meal into the radiator and also buying chewing gum at a local Kaffir store. We got there and back without any incident except we got stuck in a water splash. On Saturday I went rifle shooting at the local range. It was run by the British South African Police. I got quite a good score.

On the Sunday I rode over to lunch with one of the Hanmer family. Riding is one of the best means of transport here as the roads are few and far between. The Hanmers live about six miles from here. There are two Hanmer brothers and they own about 90,000 acres between themselves and they are into forestry in a large way. The one I visited was Charles Hanmer, the other Bill. Charles was very like Rudge Humphreys [of Usk Castle] with his interest in trees and also untidiness. He has a very nice wife.

The weather here is not unlike the British Isles cloudy and cool, but when the sun comes out it can be really warm.

When I was staying with Anthony, I had to sleep on the veranda as they have only a small cottage. It was great fun lying awake at night listening to all the noises of the bush. One of the funniest and uncouth noises was a mother baboon scolding her baby, it was a very human sound. The only snag sleeping in the open here was that my bed got full of ants.

This part of my letter will be mainly for Daddy's benefit. There is a wonderful future for a good dairy in Salisbury and I am making a survey of the markets around Rhodesia. The present dairy in Salisbury is a co-op run and financed by the government and it is terribly inefficient and nobody gets any milk in Salisbury. The town is increasing so rapidly, and there is a very large African population. The government is very worried about the malnutrition in Africans and TB is rampant. No African can afford to drink milk but I believe that the Tetra Pak machine will put milk prices within their grasp and also the prospects of flying milk from the dairying districts around Salisbury up to the copper belt where milk is practically unobtainable due to the unhealthy farming conditions. I will be interested to know how John's Tetra Pak machine is progressing. I think there is a complete goldmine out here in milk.

I am going to spend most of my stay out here studying the prospect of a plant in Salisbury. I am keeping the scheme very quiet, and I am trying to discover if there are any other concerns thinking on the same lines.

I have many letters from my friends in the UK and this week a very nice one from Lavinia Leighton [a girlfriend from London].

I have met a Michael Bishop from Crickhowell he is working for Charles Hanmer. He is a very nice person and tomorrow I have organised a party at the local hotel as Douglas Leighton Seager is coming up to stay here.

Lots of love
From Robin

Qwaraguzi
Inyanga
S. Rhodesia

June 21st 1956

Dear Mummy

Thank you for your letter also father's. Michael Posnett's engagement came as a surprise to me and I do not know the girl, as I got a bit behind with the Cheshire gossip. You will have to send me all the details.

Douglas Leighton Seager came and stayed at the local hotel for last weekend. He brought 3 girls with him. 2 of the girls I met in Capetown and they hitchhiked their way up to here. They are working their way around the world. On Saturday we explored Inyanga and the surrounding countryside. In the evening the hotel staged a dinner dance and we made a party up as Michael Bishop who I told you about in my previous letter made up the sixth. The party was a great success and the hotel certainly hadn't seen such high spirits for a long time. On Sunday Douglas brought the girls over and we all went riding and then had lunch. The Charles Hanmers also came over so we all sat down to a Rhodesian lunch.

On Wednesday I went with Anthony W. Birch to a cattle sale at a place called Rusapi not far from here. The Rhodesian sales are all in the open air and the pens are constructed out of wooden poles. This sale was very poorly attended due to not being advertised properly so the cattle went very cheaply, half the price for the same type of cows in England. Dairy cows at £22 each. All the Rhodesian farmers arrived at the sale in large American shooting brakes and pickup trucks, all wearing wide brimmed hats and mostly in shorts.

On the way here we stopped at a Roman Catholic missionary to look at some porkers. I have never seen such a set up, huge big place miles from anywhere but in a most attractive setting amid large woodlands. We arrived there in the middle of the afternoon and found the missionaries all seated at lunch! A huge affair with wine etc. they had vineyards there as well.

A Father Egan rose up to meet us. He carefully explained to us that they had their own system of time and he told us that it was God's own time they kept to. Father Egan looked just like our Rev. Davies with a fat baby face and curly hair also he was wearing a pair of blue tinted glasses. It made me very home sick to hear the Irish brogue as they are all of an Irish order.

We went and saw the pigs, some rather scraggy. As we went through the compound we passed all the numerous shrines and Virgin Marys in the rocks.

Missionaries as you well realise are not very popular out here and they are regarded to do more damage than good. The R.C.s are about the best as they discipline the Africans very well.

The weather here has been gorgeous warm and sunny. The only trouble is the dust in the dry season especially on the roads.

Today we have been dosing cattle for fluke and we had to get through nearly 300. It was very exhausting but also very amusing watching the African herd boys catching the cows.

The job I mentioned to Mr Newhouse [our bank manager from Newport] was to be a salesman in selling cattle dips etc. to farmers but I didn't take it as it would mean letting down the W. Birches after the trouble of getting me out here and also it meant finding accommodation which is rather tricky. I am not in too much of a hurry to find a situation. Yet!

I am sending a couple of cuttings in this letter for Daddy and I will send some financial papers by sea giving details of the items which he mentioned in his letter.

The building trade is very healthy at the moment in spite of recent wage increases amongst the Africans. Around Salisbury there are a large number of housing estates being built and in Salisbury itself they are demolishing old colonial buildings, and creating large blocks of offices.

Looking forward to your next letter.

Love

Robin

June 28th 1956

Dear Mummy

Thank you for your last letter. Your letters always arrive on a Monday same as they did at school.

This week I went on a trip to Umtali with Anthony W. Birch to look at some milling machinery which was for sale. It was a very interesting drive and a very pretty route as it took us all through the mountains. We left at the crack of dawn to be there in good time. The first part of the journey took us through large tracks of forestry owned by the Wattle Company of Rhodesia. Wattle is the same plant as our mimosa in the greenhouse. It grows as a weed out here.

About 10 miles from Umtali we passed a gold mining community. The first gold mine I have seen. Most of the mines were worked out so only the spoil heaps remained making the valley look very like a south Wales one with straggling townships.

We spent the morning shopping in Umtali and also we inspected the milling plant but found it unsuitable for our use. We had lunch with a friend of Anthony's who was an irrigation officer, he was a Scotsman with a large sense of humour. At lunch he mentioned about his "wee working up top of the glen" i.e. a gold mine which he was a shareholder in. It is highly illegal for a Civil Servant to run a business so he has to keep it very quiet amongst even his best friends.

After lunch we set off on a trip to visit Kingsley Fairbridge's memorial at the top of Christmas pass. We piled into Anthony friend's old Pontiac car and when it got to the top of the pass the speedometer mileage turned over to 100,000 miles. So we had a wee droppy to celebrate the occasion.

I found Umtali a most attractive town and it had the charm of an English market town also a certain continental flavour about it due to being so near the Portuguese frontier. Many Portuguese come over to shop here. The town has a most splendid situation amongst the hills.

I drove the 80 miles home to Inyanga in the Chevrolet shooting brake. I must say the big American cars are a joy to drive and cruise along effortlessly. In the 80 miles we only met two other cars such a change after England, of course one missed the good tarmac, as all the roads are primarily dirt and very dusty.

This week I have been very busy in hunting for lost cattle we are 52 short on the last count, so I have been out with search parties of African boys. The country here is very difficult to comb due to the hills, crags and large areas of forestry and also scrub. I have been riding on these searches and cover as much as 30 miles a day.

My horse is called Tit Bits, she was an ex polo pony, but she proved to be too fast to manage in the polo field. She is very like Jean to look at, as she has Exmoor blood. She is also a great character and very willing, climbs and follows me up and down the steepest places without leading her. Today I jumped over a large fence into an African Kraal and terrified all the women folk. They downed tools and fled into the shelter of their huts.

On these expeditions I have had the chance to see some of the wild life of Africa. Yesterday I disturbed a wild pig; he went off with a tremendous snort and grunt and ran off looking over his shoulder to see if I was following with his tail straight in the air. I quite often see buck. They are quite attractive as they bound over the rocks. The Africans have Kaffir dogs i.e. lurchers, hunt them but not often with success. They are very amusing whilst they last. I have seen secretary birds which strut around looking for snakes etc., they have a very dignified appearance. I have not seen any ostriches up here but I saw some in the Karroo desert in S.A.

I have noticed in Africa that I very rarely see game during the day as one would expect to see. It is surprisingly still and the birds here are not full of song, all they manage is a shrill whistle which lasts about a second then all is quiet again. Hawks are very much in evidence, so are buzzards. I have also seen Franklin partridges but not in very large coverts. Yesterday, I saw a pair of Marabou storks which stand about 5ft high and are very handsome. I have yet to see leopards, hyenas and lions but all these creatures move only at night, also such as anteaters which live in enormous burrows which would shame a badger. I have picked up porcupine quills on the ground also a snakeskin but so far no snakes. It is too cold at this time of the year for them.

I am also turning myself into an amateur geologist and have collected lots of stones. I have found deposits of mica and bauxite, also quartz. I am always on the lookout for gold which has been found in small quantities in the hills.

This country is also very interesting from the archaeologist point of view. I have come across large stone encampments and fortifications, and also the hillsides are very heavily irrigated and terraced at one time and traces still remain remarkably intact. No one knows who occupied the country but whoever did was highly civilised, far more than the present Africans who only live in stick and mud huts.

I was very amused about your story about Daddy and Major Bull and the fete. I am certain that he and Daddy ought to share a seat in parliament. And also very amused about the Jaguar car hunt. Daddy is entering into his second youth.

I hope the Italian girl is a great success. I wrote to [my sister] Vicky for her birthday.

Give my regards to the little dogs. The W. Birches have a cat with the same sort of habits as Silvers, and the same age – desperately greedy. He is a Siamese.

Lots of love

Robin

Qwaraguzi
Inyanga
S. Rhodesia

4th July 1956

Dear Mummy

Thank you for your very interesting letter. I also had a letter from
Aunt Betty Bowers. It was mainly about what Cousin Barbara had
been doing and her being taken out in London by Paddy [Kennedy].
She was also highly indignant that Barbara would be made to bathe
whilst she was in France from the threats of Daddy on your caravan
holiday.

I am again living down at Inyanga village with Anthony W. Birch
and I have now taken over the management of the dairy farm
which I am finding most interesting. This week I have been planning an irrigation scheme. A job after my own heart from my child-
hood days, canals and pipes. I have had a gang of African labourers
digging trenches but I find it very difficult trying to keep them on
a straight line and will insist in making everything crooked. I find
at times it is dealing with a lot of Turners [Turner – the Glen Usk
butler] as their intelligence is about the same level, and they do the
exact opposite to what you tell them, but on the whole I find they
are very likable and very amusing at times, and also willing. I am
learning to speak Kaffir.

I have been given a Model A Ford car to run as my personal transport about the farm. I christened the car "Beatrice" and she is a 1930
model great fun to drive, rather like my Aston Martin in build with a
semi open body, known out here as a Safari car. As I speed along the
road all the Africans stop and stare and then raise their hats to me.

During the week I have also been working at the mill as well and overhauled one of its machines for maize crushing. It is a very busy time of year as the maize is coming in off the African reserves.

The mill has also a butchers shop and the ranch cattle are sold through the shop. It is a good idea on paper but unfortunately this country is entirely on the never never system of payments and our customers are very reluctant to pay up on their bills, so it is one vicious circle as the shop cannot pay its own accounts. The attitude is that there is always tomorrow "to pay".

We are also becoming agents for farm machinery such as oxen ploughs and carts, in fact we are becoming a Kaffir store. I am having a most amusing time in selling these carts to the African farmers. They always think they have been swindled. We are also thinking of installing a petrol pump as there is considerable lorry traffic with mealies. I am most fascinated by these Africans as they own the very best lorries all bought new. One African owning a large Bedford wears a blazer and light blue trousers also a yachting cap adorns his head. When the lorry is being unloaded he stands on top of the cab shouting orders to his boys who are dressed in smart blue overalls.

When a lorry arrives from an outlying district the entire population seems to travel on it as on top of the mealie sacks. You see the most incredible sights of wives, children, chickens in baskets, cooking pots, bicycles and blankets all being unloaded and the commotion is unbelievable. I don't believe Paddington station could equal it of all the welcomes and chatter. These Africans, like Turner [butler at Glen Usk], are very dressy. They wear the most gaudy clothes but there is an old boy here who is foreman at one of the farms dresses in the style of an English gentleman farmer. He got this idea through reading Country Life and Fields seeing the style of dress. He has now blossomed out in knee britches, gaiters and a tweed hacking jacket along with a tweed cap. He is now saving his money up so he can come to England and see the sights for himself.

This weekend Anthony and two friends and myself are going camping. We have a bank holiday here and [it] is known as Rhodes and Founders. We are going to Inyanga north for an exploring trip. This part of the country is true Africa and it is low country compared with this, it is completely uninhabited except for a few African tribes which are still quite primitive. There are rumours of deposits of pitch blend from which uranium is extracted so we are going to investigate. In this part game is abundant so are lions, elephants, rhino and crocodiles in the rivers. I am taking my gun with me and quantities of ammo, also I have taken precautions against malaria. We are motoring down in the Ford V8 and also a Land Rover which belongs to a Government Conservation officer who is also taking a party of high ranking officials. We are showing them their country as Anthony knows the district quite well. I am the engineer of the party responsible for the welfare of vehicles.

I will give you a long discourse on my travels in next week's letter and also what we will find.

I had some correspondence from Bam [my father's stock broker] on Rhodesian industrial projects such as cement etc. I will reply to him as soon as I have information. One of Anthony's friends is connected with the brick industry so I hope next week I will have some information for Daddy.

There is a project here which will make quite a lot of money in the future, the Rhodesian Wattle Company. Wattle here is grown for leather tanning and plastics, the firm owns a huge acreage of trees and they are just maturing and the firm is building a new factory for processing.

I am keeping very fit and well.

Love

Robin

PS. I am enclosing a leaflet on Dairy Equipment for Daddy.

Qwaraguzi
Inyanga
S. Rhodesia

13th July 1956

Dear Mummy

Thank you very much for your two letters. I have written to the Rhodesian civil engineering firm giving details of myself etc. It may be a very good job if I am lucky enough to get it. I am very interested in your choice for Lady Raglan's party. I have met Bunny Esterhazy at the " Shropshire Hunt Club" dance last April and also there has been a lot in the papers out here about the splendour of their London party.

I must now tell you of my trip to Inyanga North. The government officials didn't turn up, I think they probably feared the bush and all the living creatures so we set off on our own in our Ford V8. There are four of us, myself Anthony W.B. and two friends of his. One was a typical army officer, incidentally a gunner, called Marcus and the other was a South African solicitor called Michael.

We all started off on Saturday after lunch. The car was fully loaded right down to the springs with all the necessary camping equipment bedding rolls, pot, pans, boxes of food and guns, fishing tackle etc. The first day's journey leads us through the foothills of the Inyanga mountains mainly past European farms of Dutch settlers. We stopped for tea on the road side at a place called Mica Hill which is named so after deposits of mica being found. I found an out crop of soapstone which is green in colour and looks and feels like soap. This stone is used for the manufacture of talc powder and baby powders, but unfortunately not economical to mine here because of transport difficulties. After Mica Hill we ran into African reserves which are put aside for Africans not allowing any white settlers in. The Africans are supervised by the Native Commissioners and Missions. We arrived at the rest camp for our first night to find it occupied by a party of young things from the Salisbury Society. They had a party of three girls and men, when we arrived and unpacked we made a point of monopolizing their camp fire over which we proceeded to grill fillet of steak. The other party were only having cooked beans so as soon as fillets began to sizzle and give out an aroma they came and hung round like a lot of vultures. We spent a very pleasant evening talking and telling stories around the fire.

When we decided to go to bed it was a sight worth seeing as we all decided to sleep in the open as the other party had monopolized the beds in the rest house.

Marcus being rather like Chris Cory very large and having everything most comfortable as possible proceeded to erect a very elaborate camp bed and also a collapsible bath complete with stopper in the bottom.

Michael on the other hand had a Lilo which he proceeded to blow up with the car pump and also a nylon sleeping bag a type designed for an Everest expedition which could fold into a small rucksack, whilst Anthony and I had only bedding rolls ex British Army – very comfortable. I covered my face with TCP to ward off mosquitoes. Marcus went to bed wearing a night cap with a tassel on the end.

You hear the most wonderful noises sleeping under the stars ranging from crickets to drums from an African compound. They were having a beer drinking sessions and dances, every so often they would let out blood curling shrieks.

We arose to a crisp African morning and cooked our breakfast over the camp fire and also Michael had a marvellous kettle called a "volcano" which had a little fire inside it like a steam engine and it could boil with most extraordinary rapidity. After breakfast we soon packed up and were once again on the road. Michael and I rode on the back of the Ford which has a truck type container instead of a normal boot. We had our guns ready for any guinea fowl. We never saw any, the only time we did we hadn't got our guns out of their cases.

The road we travelled on rapidly deteriorated and soon we came on stretches where we all had to walk. It was certainly the worst road I have ever travelled on. The number of times the car hit the bottom was uncountable and some were the most alarming smacks and the petrol tank received some huge dents. It was remarkable that it didn't leak. I must say the V8 stood it marvellously.

Our second camp was situated on a most beautiful river which was the border to Portuguese East Africa. I waded across into their territory. The road we came on was the route of the Cape to Cairo telephone line and it crossed the river just at this point. Unfortunately, there had been a hunting party up the banks of the river just previously and thus we saw nothing. The only thing seen was a large green water snake by Michael whilst he was washing in the river. He was frightened out of his wits and came running back to the camp half clothed. We also saw marks of crocodiles in the river sand and I heard an enormous splash whilst I was filling a kettle, near the opposite bank. This country is very low at 1,900 ft above sea level. At this level an extraordinary tree grows called a baobab. It looks like a gigantic turnip with branches sprouting out of the top. It dates back from prehistoric age. It is like a huge turnip more than a tree, as there is no wood, only pith. There are some photographs which I took and I will send to you as early as possible.

This river was a very swiftly flowing one as it came out of the mountains so therefore free of bilharzia which is a parasite, what gets into one's blood stream, if you bath in one of the infected rivers. When I laid awake at night I could hear the booming of rocks as they smacked each other in the current on the river bed.

On the third day we started to motor back towards Inyanga along the banks of the river. The county we passed through was quite beautiful some of the best scenery I have yet seen in Africa not very unlike the border country of Wales, with the low wooded hills and very fertile valleys with high brown mountains in the back ground.

We made our camp near a lovely mountain stream on our third night amongst tall trees and moss covered rocks. It was lovely to be lulled to sleep with the roar of water in your ears. The very fertile valleys were intensely farmed solely by Africans under European supervision and I was very impressed with them and also the crops which they got off the land. It certainly made me wonder how long the white man can farm effectively in competition with them. They were just starting on a vast irrigation project which would bring their farms under water the whole year round.

We stopped and visited an African store and I was quite amazed how well run it was and also how clean and tidy the whole place seemed to be. He also owned two lorries and a van in connection with his business, a lot of African farms had motor vehicles of sorts. Another point I find a problem to reason with is that when these Africans build a store which are often a sizable building the owners still prefer to live in their stick and mud huts beside the store. On our fourth day we left the fertile valleys and climbed 4,000 ft into the Inyanga hills and how cold it was after the warm valleys we covered over 200 miles in all, and a most pleasant trip.

Marcus works for a Salisbury brick firm and the information I got out of him was that demand for bricks was far greater than the supply and no brick firm bothers itself to run as an efficient unit. When I next go to Salisbury I am going to be shown round the brickworks. I am starting up my irrigation project this week. I have definitely decided that pigs are the best livestock to have in this country, the way more have put on weight.

Lots of love,

Robin

23rd July 1956

Dear Mummy

I am afraid this may be a rather hurried letter as my usual Sunday letter period has been taken up with a lot of work in connection with our new church. Today we had the consecration service and had the Archbishop down for the occasion. During the week I spent a lot of time helping in last minute preparations and super-vising local boys in laying out the road up to the church, and also, I spent some time on the top of a rickety ladder cleaning the chancel window removing all the putty finger marks.

The church has been erected out of local funds. It is mainly the work of three of the original settlers at Inyanga. Charles Hanmer gave the land and provided the wood for the roof and porch. A family called Pearce helped and supervised the building and also the Wyrley Birches helped a lot with the work. Charles Hanmer's mother provided a lot of the funds and the design was based on their family church in England. It is very attractive, as it is a Norman design and made of the local stone which has a rather nice mellow colour, almost sandstone. Unfortunately, the weather let us down as it rained. It is actually supposed to be the dry season, but Inyanga being so high it is very much wetter and a more temperate climate. It can also be very cold.

The setting might have been somewhere in Scotland with the mist and drizzle. We had planned to have tea in the open after the ceremony but it was cancelled so I spent Sunday morning moving

29

all the equipment to our local hotel in a little Ford van, like my one, which I had been kindly lent for the occasion.

We had lunch at the house of the Pearce family. The Archbishop was late so we waited and waited and eventually he arrived after thumbing a lift. The wheel had come off his car on the way up to Inyanga. Then he hurriedly had his lunch and we all departed for the church. The Archbishop is called Paget and is the brother of the General. He also had a great sense of humour.

The funniest item of the day was there were several babies christened. These babies had been turned down by the local vicar as one was from a divorcee and the other a Rastafarian? The Vicar here like our Rev. Davies is very narrow minded and objected to any other denominations except Anglicans. So the anxious parents in desperation asked the Archbishop to baptise them as there is no other parish within 60 miles. One girl was 6 years old and parents had been waiting all this time.

When the babies were christened the Vicar had to look on much to every bodies amusement.

After the service we departed off to the local hotel which is incidentally a very good one and we all sat down to a slap up tea and cream cakes and listened to the usual back slapping of speeches, the Archbishop had us all in fits of laughter over his brief address. That evening we had a dinner party at Qwaraguzi and the local lay preacher who is also a doctor came and kept us very well entertained with shaggy dog stories.

I am now writing this letter from Maradellas on the way to Salisbury. I am going up there this week on business for the Wyrley Birches and also a dentist visit as I chipped a tooth the other day.

I am staying at the farm of the W. Bs' eldest daughter who is married to a farmer owning a 2,000 acre dairy farm, unfortunately I arrived in the dark so I haven't seen round the premises yet.

They are both very horsey and have about 20 horses and are very keen on polo. Maradellas is rather like the Beaufort Country, as home to many monied horse loving people of Rhodesia.

There is a very good Polo Club but no hunting of any sort. The county is well suited for it as being predominately grassland with rolling hills.

On the way up I had Mrs Wyrley Birche's grandchildren ages 5 and 6 and also a Hanmer relation and Hanmer daughter returning to school. One of the children was very sick on the way and we had to make numerous stops. I enjoy driving on the Rhodesian roads as one meets very little traffic and also the roads are straight with no hedges to block one's vision.

I will tell you all about my Salisbury trip in my next letter.

With lots of love

Robin

Qwaraguzi
Inyanga
S. Rhodesia

29th July 1956

Dear Mummy

Thank you very much for your two letters of the week. I was most interested in your letter of Lady Raglan's party I am sorry that your debs didn't come up to scratch. I am sure that Lady Raglan must have profited from her experiences of organising dances in the past to make the dance such a success.

I had a most enjoyable three days in Salisbury. I went up by myself from Maradellas early on Wednesday morning and spent the day doing business for the Wyrley Birches. Salisbury is a very well planned city as each commodity has premises in its own area. The farming and machinery suppliers have one block to themselves so if you can't get what you want at one shop you only need to go a few doors down to try at another establishment. All this helped a lot with my shopping.

Salisbury is now lined with the new parking meters in the centre of the city. The reason is to prevent office and shop keepers from parking their cars all day outside their premises. It is worked at 1/- for two hours and sixpence for an hour. At one time I managed to obtain forty minutes free time as the car in front moved away before his time.

The Salisbury shops are very good except for clothes etc., and I found you can get everything else that you wanted.

In the evening I went out to Salisbury's most elite nightclub known as the Coq d'Or. I was very impressed with it and very reasonable compared with London equivalent. When we were seated for dinner

I saw a very familiar face at the next table to mine. After a while my curiosity was roused and I went over to speak to the girl and she was one I had met at Cirencester in my beagling days. This is such a small world, we all joined up and made one large and very joyful party.

The next day I had lunch at the Sports Club of Salisbury where the polo grounds are. It is the most beautiful laid out for all sports, there are pitches for rugger and cricket as well. My trip off to the dentist went very well and my tooth didn't actually have a hole only what is known as a soft spot and was easily treated by applying a chemical solution. Unfortunately, this country has no national health scheme but this is beneficial to a fit person like myself, but hospitals can be expensive if one requires treatment.

When I visited Salisbury I called on Stewarts and Lloyds as I had to buy irrigation equipment for the dairy farm. S and L's have just opened up a new depot in connection with selling steel pipes and irrigation equipment, both have good sales in this country.

I also had an interview with the manager of the African Investment Trust Ltd and asked him about the prospects of investment in the federation. He told me that Rhodesian Brick and Potteries and Rhodesian Portland Cement are the safest industrial investments as they are controlled by very good managers. He also told me that so many Rhodesian concerns sound a good proposition on paper but unfortunately fall down over the management side.

The most popular type of investment is property and I am not surprised by the building activity. Many people are prepared now to own a town flat than to live out in the suburbs where they have to motor in each day with the rush hour traffic and then to be faced with a parking problem. Also, suburban houses are becoming costly to maintain due to rises in wages of African house boys and garden boys. The cost of living is rising rapidly like any other part of the world and the standard of living is as high as America. Every person owns a car and most families have two or three. The number of cars in the federation equals the whole population.

I have written a long letter to Bam giving details of investments. A new Rhodesian firm is coming on the market shortly that is like

CBR engineering. It is the result of amalgamating several small firms. One is Bentalls the agricultural machinery firm one time connected with the British firm of the same name; they are well established in the federation. This firm is going to have the agency for Perkins diesel engines and Seddon diesel lorries.

During my visit to Salisbury I paid some visits to self service shops of groceries and meat. They were more advanced than anything I have seen in England. All the meat and vegetables were packed in cellophane bags on refrigerated counters each labelled and priced. Mrs Wyrley Birch says she has met Mrs Bramwell and she bought a puppy from her for her mother when she was last in England. Her mother used to live near Timewell House in Devon. I enjoyed your report about Silverstone, I had completely forgotten about it as I don't ever see the motor papers out here. We live in another world as they say.

One of the dogs has just had puppies very suddenly without any signs what so ever, at first we thought she was ill and then suddenly produced six puppies in the night. We have six hound puppies which have reached the naughty age. They remind me so much of Stella and Starlight. There is also a sweet little dachs its mother died during birth and was brought up on a bottle by Mr W. Birch's eldest daughter. It is just like our Gemma, pools everywhere. This country is marvellous for children as they can always play out of doors throughout most of the year. Everyone has at least three children and they run wild without any shoes or clothing about the farms, they are extraordinary healthy except they do get bilharzia sometimes if they come in contact with an infected stream.

One night whilst in Maradellas I went and visited a farm nearby owned by a young English couple. The man was a split image of Geoffrey Somerset and had the same sort of sense of humour. He was busy planting his farm with gum trees for there is to be a Rayon factory to be erected in Maradellas and gum is very suitable.

Lots of love

Robin

Qwaraguzi
Inyanga
S. Rhodesia

4th August 1956

Dear Mummy

I have had a very busy week on the farm as I have taken on 40
more cattle for temporary purposes until they are sold next week.
My time was taken up by arranging accommodation and moving
feeding stuffs. I have also been increasing my irrigation acreage on
my scheme to cater for the increased population. I am expecting
some baby pigs at the end of the month. During the week I got
8 Kaffir pigs from an African. They are the first cousin to the wild
pig and look identical, short and round, hairy and a long snout.

The question of the Suez Canal is on every bodies lips out here
as it very much plays a part in the economy of this country's eastern
ports in Portuguese East Africa. At present only time will tell.

We get a very good news bulletin from the BBC London which
gives us details of world affairs in general. We otherwise only get
a weekly paper as Inyanga is too far off the beaten track for every
day delivery. From the bulletins we gather that you have had appalling
weather and I became quite anxious about our hay crop, did we
manage to get any at all? The weather here is quite different cold
nights with hard frosts and warm and sunny during the day. When
I get up I have to wear at least two jerseys but at midday I am only
in shirt sleeves. The range in temperatures is terrific. I rather like
it as when I feel cold I know I will be warm soon and when too
hot I look forward to the cool evening. The sunsets are quite marvellous with the wonderful colourings especially on the mountains

which turn from red to a dark purple. The sky is now becoming cloudy during the afternoon indicating the approaching rainy season. The rain usually come at the end of September that is our so called spring from now onwards each afternoon will become cloudier and cloudier with thunder but no rain and suddenly it will come down.

Last year the tea estate which is next to our land had 100 inches of rain between September and April. When it rains here it really does.

I have got my photographs back from printing today and they have come out exceedingly well. They are of the first part of the trip. I will send them to you by sea as they are too heavy by air. I think of taking up photography seriously as a hobby as Africa lends itself with sunrise etc. and I am hoping to treat myself to a better camera.

I am very pleased as I have been paid a bonus wage for the extra work I have done since I started. It will be a great help towards my new camera.

On the 17th August I am going down to Umtali for their Agricultural show. Mrs Wyrley Birch is going to judge horses. I will be very interested to see how it compares with the English ones. The Salisbury show is not until the 10th September.

Today I went down to the African reserves with our lorry to collect a load of beans. The lorry is the same as our Ford four wheel drive and on the way back a valve burnt out and I just managed to limp back to the mill. It took most of the day to travel 20 miles but I was very relieved to get home as the road is much unfrequented by any motor vehicles or Europeans, and went through deserted country. Everybody has to have great trust in their cars out here as a breakdown can be very inconvenient especially out in the bush some ten to twenty miles to the nearest phone let alone a garage.

I must end now as it is nearing my bed time. 9.00 pm like Granny Head.

Lots of love

From Robin

Qwaraguzi
Inyanga
S. Rhodesia

17th August 1956

Dear Mummy

I haven't had any news of your holiday yet but I expect that the French mail is not up to our standards.

We are enjoying lovely weather and it gets quite warm during the day. Last Sunday I rode to the top of Rhodesia's highest mountain Inyangani 8,200 ft. It is about a 10 mile ride from here I was very lucky as it was a beautifully fine day without a cloud in the sky.

A lot of the time the mountain has its head shrouded in cloud. It was an easy ride up except in one part where I had to dismount and lead 'Tip Toes' through scrub. On the slopes I saw a lot of game such as buck and various hawks and eagles and also dassies. I managed to ride within 10 ft of the summit. Once on the top I had the marvellous views over the Portuguese territory, seven thousand feet below me. It was just like being in an aeroplane seeing rivers winding their way over the planes towards the coast. On the Rhodesian side there was only a 3,000 ft drop as it was the plateau of central Africa.

It was a little bit hazy as this time of the year the atmosphere becomes thick with dust and smoke from the many veldt fires. The best time is just after the rains in March.

During the week I have been installing another water scheme on the dairy farm and also Anthony WB and I have been busy repairing

37

cars and lorries, as we only had one working out of five, all the others had some malady.

I am now living in Inyanga village at a guest house as Anthony's wife Susan is shortly expecting a baby so I have moved out for a while.

On Thursday I went with Mrs W. Birch to Umtali for the Show. On the way down she took me to see various famous tourist attractions which Rhodesia has to offer. The Dunguare gorge a most magnificent sight with a waterfall at its head and then a 1,000 ft gash in the plateau making a narrow valley out into the Portuguese territory, and also we visited a waterfall which drops down to 2,000 ft over the escarpment of the eastern highlands. The most amazing part was that the drop was so great that the water never reached the bottom, it dissolved before getting there. I must say that both Anthony and Mrs W. Birch are the most entertaining travelling companions as they know all about the districts and the local inhabitants which we passed through.

On Friday night we stayed just outside Umtali with the manager of the Sheba timber estate. This estate is financed by various members of the British Aristocracy; one is Lord Forester from Shropshire. There is about 12,000 acres of timber growing.

The manager's name was Roberts and his wife came from Donnington in Shropshire. They had a lovely house and garden with a swimming pool situated in the forest.

They also had a baby buck as a pet it was reared on a bottle. It was really the most attractive pet I have seen yet. It was tame as a dog and you could stroke it. During the evening it lay in front of the fire chewing its cud and at supper it had a bowl of milk which it drank along with the cat. During the daytime it lived in a run out in the garden.

On Saturday morning we left early for the Show as Mrs W. Birch was judging children's ponies. I spent the morning shopping in Umtali. I have been very attracted to Umtali and the shops were surprisingly good. The weather has warmed up as we are entering our spring and it was quite hot in Umtali which is a good bit lower than here. I had lunch on the Showground. The Show was the size of Monmouth show and not very much stock, what there was, was surprisingly good. Some very nice Angus, no Guernseys, a few Jerseys and mainly Friesians and also African breeds.

They had classes for pigs and sheep. The exhibitors were mainly estate development companies and a few private individuals. Umtali is not really a farming district, mainly forestry because of the hilly nature of the country. I also saw a very good film on government irrigation projects in some of the bigger river valleys. I am considering of buying a Land Rover and going to visit some of the schemes. It is amazing what can be grown with water, fertile soil and hot sun. Anything from wheat to bananas.

The produce was very good and so were the flowers as you have an inexhaustible supply out here to choose from. There were home craft exhibits and young farmers produce also they had photography and art etc.

There was a dog tent and poultry. The dog owners like the English counterparts look just like their dogs.

After the show Mrs W Birch took me to see an old friend of hers who lived on the way back to Inyanga. These people were descended from the Meikle family who were one of the early pioneers and made a fortune out of stores and hotels.

It is far the most attractive part of Rhodesia I have yet seen. The house was situated overlooking a beautiful lush green valley with a mountain behind. The house was surrounded by a beautiful garden and tall gum trees. When crossed the threshold of the house it went back to 1907 as it was furnished and built in that period. The furnishings was typical antimacassars, basket chairs, old family photographs and heavy mahogany furniture, also, venetion [sic] blinds and velvet curtains with curtain rods with large brass knobs. Two old sisters lived there, one was 92 and bedridden the other 87 and still ran the farm.

We only just managed to reach Qwaraguzi as the old V8 developed ignition troubles and we only were running on 4 of the 8 cylinders.

Lots of love

From Robin

PS. Can you obtain for me my bank statements for the months of April and May as they are holding up my accounting.

Qwaraguzi
Inyanga
S. Rhodesia

August 1956

Dear Mummy

Thank you for your London letter. I was glad that your tenants had left everything in order in the flat. I am most interested to hear all about the caravan trip and the places where you had visited.

I have had another busy week with the farming etc. Last Thursday I attended an African cattle sale organised by the Native Development. The meat trade has just been decontrolled in this county in the last 3 months and this was the first time a sale of this nature had been held.

I had a most entertaining day as the Native Development had not a clue how to run a sale. It was supposed to start at 9.00 am but it was delayed until 12.00 before the first cow was put through the ring. At the start they found the scales for weighing were too small and a bullock got stuck and the scales had to be dismantled to remove him amongst a lot of excited local Africans.

Then cattle kept on escaping out of the pens and disappearing over the veldt. The pens were only constructed out of flimsy poles in which the white ants had been busy.

Whilst the sale was in progress and the prices seemed fairly reasonable the African onlookers rushed off to their kraals to bring back their odd cow to be sold so all through the sale cattle came in dribs and drabs.

Buying and selling was all in cash for the Africans' benefit and the purchasers had to pay a deposit beforehand. The sale was

41

conducted in the open air and the clerk had a desk under a fig tree but a squall of wind came and swept all the notes and money off his desk across the sale ground into various people's pockets.

Whilst the sale was in progress Anthony WB spotted a cow with his own brand and ear mark, so we started to make inquiries and the police got busy but it had no owner. I imagine the owner realising what had happened decided to disown it, so we got it back.

In the early part of the week we had serious trouble from hyena attacks. On Monday night they took two lambs and a calf, they dug their way into the pens. The second night they killed three ewes in spite of that we had chained dogs around the kraal. Then they came back again on the fourth day only taking one ewe.

We took the trouble of laying traps and poison but they are too cunning and have the uncanny way of avoiding the tempting baits.

The Native Department has a new method of combating the menace by using detonators hidden in a bone of a piece of meat and used as bait, when the hyena crunches the bone the detonator goes off and virtually blows the beast to pieces. One has to use these drastic measures with hyena and leopards as they do the most appalling damage to livestock.

In the middle of last night I was roused by the furious barking of dogs and went out with my gun to investigate but all was quiet with the sheep. It must have been a prowler awaiting his chance.

In your last letter you mentioned about plans for the future. At the moment I am being fairly well paid at a rate of £6 to £7 a week in addition to my board and lodgings and I am also gaining valuable experience here in handling African labour.

I hope you all have a lovely holiday and the weather is fine.

Lots of love

Robin

PS. I have sent you off my photographs.

Dear Mummy

An Air card this week as I have run out of my note paper. I got the second letter from France this week. I was very amused to read that Daddy flew home for a weekend!

I have had another week busy at the books as the accountant who had malaria has gone away for his father's funeral and also we had more car trouble and Anthony and I have got bits of car littered all over the butchery. We have two Ford V8s with broken chassis.

The other day I received a magnificent book on the Zambezi River by post at first I pondered over who was the sender. It turned out to be one of the old ladies who I found broken-down on the road near here and I repaired their car for them. It is typical of the generosity this country has to offer.

During the week Nigel W. Birch had his second birthday. He had a small birthday party and lots of presents. I gave him a clock-work mini car, he is a charming little boy and very typically grubby and naughty at times.

I am expecting some little pigs and I have some sows coming down within the next fortnight. I have just finished the maternity home for them and also I have finished the water scheme and now have piped water to all the buildings. It is very amusing to watch the Africans trying a tap for the first time. They stand around each turning it on in turn. One enterprising one looked up the spout and another turned it on and the African boy got a face full of water.

Wonders never cease as we had rain last night. I woke up hearing the patter on the roof and the distant roll of thunder. The country smelt lovely and fresh, and today we had another storm with hail-stones as large as mothballs. These storms are the precursor to the actual rainy season doesn't begin until the end of October.

The rain came just in time as Qwaraguzi was running short of water. We are now entering my second spring, all the blossoms are out and the bush is beginning to freshen up on the whole the countryside is looking very attractive.

With lots of love

Robin

P.O Inyanga

9th September 1956

Dear Mummy

Thank you very much for your last letter and also thank Vicky [my sister Victoria] for her most amusing one and I so enjoyed the drawings. I was very interested to read about your proposing to come out here in February, incidentally February here is rather wet as it is in the middle of the rainy season. March is a better month or April when the rains are over.

I suggest that you either come out by sea to Cape Town and then I could meet you and motor or fly up through the Union to Johannesburg then on to Salisbury or otherwise fly out to Salisbury and then go south to the Cape then home by sea.

I have just got back from my trip to Salisbury for the show. Salisbury is just like Dublin for show week. Crowds of people and great festivity all over the city in the way of dances etc., I went to two parties which were great fun. The show ground is permanent and most beautifully laid out with avenues of trees and the stands are all permanently created so are the grandstands and members enclosures. I was very kindly given a member's ticket by the Wyrley Birches so I had a seat in the stand almost next to the Governor General's box. I only had Saturday to attend the show as Friday I was busy doing business for my firm and also trying to sell one of their cars which I failed to do as there is a slump in the second-hand car market here.

The show was about the size of the Three Counties and there

was good stock entries especially of the Guernseys, some were rather indifferent and some were good. The prize winning bull was specially imported from England and he was a Roselad. The Angus were well supported mostly exhibited by Scotsmen farming out here. There was a tremendous entry for the pig classes. They had a landrace section in as well.

I met a great friend of mine who used to live with me at Ludlow House Tetbury. He has also come out here, working on a farm near Salisbury and he was looking after 40 pigs at the show! He managed to leave his pigs in the afternoon and toured the show with me so we spun a few yarns about our Cirencester days. In the evening he and I made a party up and visited one of Salisbury's exclusive night spots.

During the afternoon I watched with my friend Michael Lamb some of the ring events. Show jumping was quite a good standard. I was disgusted with one competitor who wore a pink coat along with brown boots but one has to accept these sort of things out here. There was also a dog parade. They were all trotted in front of us on leads as each dog passed the commentator gave a discourse on its merits. The commentator was reading from a printed form and at one stage the numbers got mixed up and he started to discuss a bull terrier when a greyhound was passing the box. The same thing happened when the car parade was in progress, one of the large super American cars broke down and it held up the procession so the car behind it pushed it out of the ring amidst clapping and cheering by everyone.

The afternoon was finished up by a very good display done by the B.S.A. Police, they had Africans for a gymnastic display and then a musical ride done by the mounted police which was extremely good. They had also the police band made up entirely of Africans. When the band was playing all the Africans opposite in their enclosure got fearfully excited and started to dance about singing and clapping their hands to keep in tune.

On Friday night I went to a party given for an engagement celebration of a girl I knew when I was at Cirencester and her fiancé also came from those parts. The party went off very well and I was astonished how much was consumed in the way of drink as it is so much cheaper out here and every one only drinks "long ones" due to the climate. I will give you news about my Salisbury trip in next week's letter.

Lots of love

From Robin

Qwaraguzi
Inyanga
S.R.

12th September 1956

Dear Granny

Thank you very much for your letter, I feel that I am also guilty of letting the time pass!

Both my parents seemed to have enjoyed the caravan trip in France and my mother and Victoria sent very good descriptive letters out to me here describing the route and places where they visited. I am still amazed how they all fitted into the caravan.

I am really liking this country and what it has to offer, also, the climate to mind is perfect and the most amazing thing that it never gets too hot. I found in England last summer the temperatures were far more unbearable than out here. The most pleasant part of it is that the nights are always cool and cold on occasions with frosts. We are now entering the rainy season and already have had a few storms and the countryside has become green overnight and all the dust has been laid.

Last week I went up to Salisbury for the agricultural show. The show is held on a permanent ground and is beautifully laid out amongst avenues of trees. I also had the chance to meet some of my friends who I had met when I was at Cirencester whilst I was in Salisbury, I went to two dances one was an engagement party of a girl I knew who lived in Cheltenham. Salisbury is very good for shopping and one can get almost everything which you require. The city itself is beautifully laid out. I found the streets are so wide that it is a risky business to cross them and I often find myself breaking into a run dodging the traffic. All the flowering trees and shrubs are beginning to come out as it is our spring here and Salisbury is quite lovely at present with the avenues of jacarandas breaking into flower.

In this country people have the most wonderful gardens which flower all the year round and can be kept in very good order by African garden boys.

At the moment I am on my own running the farm as the Wyrley Birches have gone away for a few days. The farm is going very well and I have just had 65 little pigs last weekend and they are all doing well and I have also got my boss boy back as he had been away on holiday and now getting on with the spring cultivations. I am going to sow a lot of potatoes this year.

On Friday the Governor General is coming down to Inyanga for a visit and I think we are all going to the reception. We are killing a special bullock for the occasion.

I am keeping very fit and well.

With best wishes

Love Robin

P.O. Inyanga

15th September 1956

Dear Mummy

Thank you very much for your two letters and the very well drawn map of your route across France and also the cutting about "terriers" which was very interesting. Unfortunately, little dogs are not successful out here due to the numerous misfortunes which happened to them in the way of diseases and wild animals etc.

You also mention in your letter about magazines. I get a chance to see all the English periodicals as the Wyrley Birches take Horse and Hound, Field etc. so you needn't send anything, but I would like a sort of commentary on our farming aspect. We keep on hearing on the news about the appalling weather in England and I wonder if we have any corn left at all. Whilst on the discussion on farming I have now 66 little pigs born into the world from my five sows all in the last week all averaging over ten so I am very pleased. They are all doing well; this is a wonderful climate for pigs. I have also had a cow calving down which has helped the milk. Tonight Anthony's dog Laura had 12 puppies unfortunately they were crossed with a boxer and she is an Alsatian so I had to take drastic measures and only two remain. The cat is also expecting kittens.

During the week I have been on my own as Anthony and his wife have taken a deserving holiday and I have been running the butchery and farm myself. The other incident of importance that Col Wyrley Birch is selling everything up if he can find a buyer at his price so my future is uncertain depending on how quickly the property is sold. I think a land company may buy for selling off into lots for building holiday cottages.

On Thursday I went to a cocktail party at the African Commissioners for Inyanga district. He has a lovely house with a swimming pool in the garden. This country does its Civil Servants with the fine Indian style. At this cocktail party I was supposed to meet the Governor General but he went on another route for Inyanga North Reserve where he has the annual meeting of the chiefs. We had to kill a special fat bullock and a sheep for his benefit.

The African Commissioner told us a very good story about the bathroom suite installed at the rest camp, everyone is highly indignant up here who works in the African department because most of them only have a hut down the garden. One secretary at the African department had to burn hers down as a snake had taken up residence in it. The village is still laughing about it as she was a woman rather a Miss Earl type – very proper!

At the rest camp on the riverside where I stayed when we went down there. The N/D installed a w/c without a chain to pull but a wheel to turn to flush the w/c. The N/D thought the governor would be more at home with this system as he is a naval man. He is Rear Admiral Paulet he is very unpopular out here at present.

On the way back from Salisbury I visited the scene of one of Rhodesia's worst rail disasters. Two goods trains collided in the night and two drivers were killed also four new diesel electric engines were a complete write off doing £25,000 of damage. Trucks were strewn twenty yards from the tracks. Some of the cattle for Salisbury show were killed. There was a truck full of new Land Rovers tossed up in the air and there was a long line of smashed Land Rovers marking the flight of this wagon, I took several photographs to record the incident.

I have had another batch of photographs printed and I hope to get them off to you fairly soon.

I am considering starting a banking account at Barclays in Salisbury as I am saving about £20 a month and I do not want to have to buy a suitcase for putting it all in?

Whilst I was in Salisbury I met again some financiers and stock-brokers and I discussed some of the schemes I had in mind. They recommended to me to wait for at least four years in this country before starting an enterprise of any sort. They recommend something in the way of a cash business as so many firms are crippled by having to carry so much credit trade.

I am in favour of self service stores in the growing suburbs of Salisbury and also this country lacks a good ice cream such as Walls. It is amazing how Coca Cola has got a hold out here. Every Kaffir store sells it no matter where you go it even has penetrated into the most remote reserves in the country. I have been most impressed by the shops run by Greeks and Italians all beautifully clean, efficient and a service with a smile and courtesy.

I have been taken up with the Suez situation and never miss a news bulletin and every night I tune into foreign stations broadcasting in English. Tonight for instance I listened to Radio Japan, the other night Radio India before Germany. We have short wave radios which can pick up these stations. It is most interesting listening to the different opinions.

I made up a little song it goes as such: Dictators may come, Dictators may go, but may the British Empire go on forever?

I am very amused about your visit to the film about Africa. I find Africa just as easy to live in as Britain; one very rarely sees the snakes and wild animals. I have killed tarantula spider on the farm all I did was to put my foot on it as any other spider. I must admit it was huge and very slow moving. I haven't seen a snake yet only two small dead ones of a harmless species. On the whole I walk around the country without ever thinking about them except I keep a lookout whilst walking through bush or long grass. The only dangers one has to be aware of are bilharzia and malaria.

They are the two scourges of Africa. I enjoyed your description of Theodore's party, I never realised that he was quite as old as that.

Lots of love

From Robin

P.O. Inyanga

30th September 1956

Dear Mummy

I expect you have been hearing about the state of emergency in S. Rhodesia over the rail strike, but it proved to be quite unnecessary as only two depots came out on strike and the trains ran normally. The strike is over now so is the state of emergency. We were a little worried here as we depend so on the railway lorries for delivering our goods, but they were unaffected by the strike.

Our cold snap that we just had is at last over, it was so cold I had to wear my polo neck sweater all day! One is so dependent on the sun at these heights and if it is cloudy it can really be cold. The frost has damaged some of the fruit blossom and blackened some of the garden plants.

During the week I have got on with the farming programme and at last our seed potatoes have come. They are rather poor, small sample of seed but it is all that we could get as potatoes are very short due to serious blight last season. The pigs are very well and growing rapidly. The little one which I have got on a bottle now laps milk from a dish now. It has got over its injuries and can walk quite well. I have made it a run at the back of Anthony's house with a small box for its bed. It has become quite tame. As soon as it has had its milk it retires for a nap in the box burying itself amongst sacking and hay to only a pink snout appears. It is a most amusing pet and now has become quite tame. It loves having his tummy scratched, I have christened him Piglet from Winnie the Pooh books.

During the rail strike the government had special broadcasts for Africans on the radio and my boss boy had been listening to them, so during milking one evening I had to explain the system of government on which this country is run. He asked me what democracy meant! We also have lengthy discussions on religion he is very keen on his church and tomorrow I have to get up earlier than usual so he can finish milking in order to attend his church service. He is the most charming boy and very intelligent, and also he will use his own initiative in doing jobs and very rarely needs to be told twice to do a thing. He would certainly show up our gillies.

On Thursday I had to take one of our lorries to the local garage which is incidentally 20 miles from here for an overhaul. This garage is kept by a German, he is an ex SS soldier typically German just like Martin Toph [our estate carpenter in Wales] about the same age, and also has a little son like Martin's over indulged with toys and sweets. When I arrived at the garage I sat down to a second breakfast as they had theirs at 10 in the morning consisting of black sausages and thick black coffee. Typically German in the way that he works practically all night as well as the day in the garage, he is a first class mechanic and is a great boon to the district.

The fishing season starts on Monday and the hotels are filling up with the fishy folk. Anthony W. Birch is very keen and he knows of the best stretches of river around here. Fishing is about 5/- a day on the main rivers. I hope to get out myself on the next week or two. That is one of the reasons I am keen on getting a Land Rover.

I must thank you for sending a friend of mine's letter from Scotland. He is another one who is thinking of coming out here. I have had several enquiries from Cirencester students about job prospects.

I must end now as it is my bed time – like Granny Head I choose 9.00 pm as I get up at 6.00 am.

Lots of love

From Robin

P.O. Inyanga

1st October 1956

Dear Mummy

I was glad to hear that you succeeded in getting all our harvest in after the depressing news we have heard on the English radio broadcasts.

I am delighted to hear your proposal to fly out in February. If you will let me know in good time the dates I will go ahead in making preparations such as hotel bookings etc. at this end. Flying out here is so simple and quick and numerous people I have met think nothing of nipping back to England for a month or so or even a week? Sea voyaging is looked upon as a tonic for health reasons.

The fishing season is well under way and on the first morning I had trout for breakfast: they were rainbow. Anthony went out early on the opening morning and caught three between ½ to 1lb each. I haven't been out yet as I have been on duty or this weekend as Anthony has gone away. I hope to start out next weekend. Inyanga is full of fishing folk for the opening week. All day large American shooting brakes cruise up and down the road carrying the rich Salisbury business men to and from the Rhodes estate where the rivers are stocked. On the opening day one man jumped in the swimming bath on the estate as he said he saw a large trout whilst he was bathing there a few months back. I haven't heard that he caught it.

On Wednesday I went and sprayed some of Col Wyrley Birch's

cattle down on one of his ranches in the low country. The temperature was well over 100 degrees. I was using a special dip called Coopertox which is very powerful for killing ticks. I managed to do 160 herd in the day with a hand spray pump.

Col W. Birch told me that he had five prospective buyers enquiring from England and one from Rhodesia and one from the Union of S.A. Mrs Wyrley Birch wants to keep some of the land in order to build a holiday cottage for the family. Forestry is the most likely use for the land or dividing the land into plots for holiday cottages.

On Thursday I had one of the most interesting experiences of my lifetime. I attended a séance. The hotel keeper and his wife are members of a spiritualist group in Salisbury and they had some other members staying in the hotel so they decided to hold a séance. I with my interest in such things asked if I could attend and they all agreed. So we all adjoined [sic] to the manager's room and seated ourselves around a table and on the table there was an upturned glass then ringing the rim the letters of the alphabet with 'yes' and 'no' along with them. We worked in groups of three and I was in the first group. One person sat out to record the messages as they came. We kept the lights on so there was no cheating! At the word go we then placed one finger on the top of the upturned tumbler and the leader said, "Is there anyone with us tonight please." I found out that you have to be very polite to the spirits unless they easily take offence. About two minutes after the glass began to oscillate gradually increasing to such a pitch that I could hardly keep my finger on the top. Then the glass came to rest in front of 'yes' on the board. Then the spokesman said, "Who would you like to communicate with tonight?" Then the glass started to move again round the board. Starting with the letter R then D, E, A, N – by that time my hair was practically standing on end. Then I had to ask the questions as the spirit wished to communicate with me. So I asked "From whom do you have a message for me, please." Then it first spelt out G.C. Dean, Uncle Geoff. It asked if I had a relative of that name, the answer was yes. Then I asked has he a message for me, the answer was No. So then who has a message for me? The tumbler then spelt out F. Dean (Daddy). By then I was desperately wanting to know what the message was, but to my disappointment it was illegible. Did Daddy have something on his mind over the date of the 5th? I feel the distance must have been too much for the spirit. So that terminated my sitting. The next three proved very successful.

One man called Fred had a message reading "Fred! give dad more room: God bless you all – from Sandra." I feel that Fred's father had been buried in a too small a coffin! Then the spirit finished up with "Go to bed Fred!" much to every bodies amusement. Since that service my belief in spiritual happenings has been strengthened considerably and I have been earmarked as a likely medium. The man called Fred was an artist so I feel those sorts of people are most likely to be selected.

There is no doubt a lot of truth in it and the amazing part that only the hotelier and his wife knew my name and they weren't taking part in it so there could not be any fiddling. No one could have possibly known Daddy's or Uncle Geoff's initials.

I have been asked to attend some of the Salisbury meetings when they have séances in the dark and the spirits play trumpets painted with luminous paint and jingle bells.

I always enjoy my Sunday letter writing as I always listen to some very good symphony concerts on the radio. The one thing I miss out here is music.

I just had a tricky problem to deal with as the garden boy here has threatened to murder his mistress as she had been unfaithful to him. Her brother has just brought her to the house along with the garden boy. They have been squabbling on the grass outside the back of the house shouting abuse at one another. I gather from the language that the garden boy had led his mistress to a secluded spot in the woods and shown her the spot where he had dug a grave to bury her after an execution. At this she took flight and bolted to the seclusion of her brother's kraal. So I have put the matter in police hands.

Top left: On the road to Inyanga North. *(Page 27)*

Top right: Cooking breakfast, Inyanga North campsite (*Left to right:* Michael, Marcus Orpen, Anthony Wyrley Birch). *(Page 26)*

Middle: Collision between two freight trains on the stretch of line between Rusape and Umtali Rhodesian Railways. *(Page 51)*

Bottom: The mill and butchery, Inyanga. (*Left to right:* Ernest Chimboza, Anthony Wyrley Birch). *(Page 23)*

Top: My faithful Series 1 Land Rover negotiating a 'Bush Road' in the Eastern Highlands. *(Page 67)*

Middle: Susan Wyrley Birch, Anthony Wyrley Birch, Young Nigel Wyrley Birch, Laura the dog. *(Page 15)*

Bottom: Anthony and Sue Wyrley Birch's cottage with its English garden, Inyanga village. *(Page 15)*

Top: The new irrigation scheme under construction utilising old water courses of an ancient civilisation which lived in the Inyanga district. The area is covered with the remains of ancient buildings, stone forts and hillside terraces similar to those seen in Southern Arabia. *(Page 22)*

Middle: Dairy cows being milked by hand, Inyanga Farm. *(Page 55)*

Bottom: Tiptoes, my polo pony, at the summit of Mt. Inyangani, at 8,500 feet the highest mountain in Southern Rhodesia. *(Page 37)*

There's no loco but trip rolls on

THE non-arrival of a steam train booked specially for a journey to celebrate the High Sheriff of Gwent's year in office failed to dampen spirits on Saturday.

Guests of Robin Dean, the High Sheriff of Gwent, for the afternoon trip to Shrewsbury and back included council leaders, businessmen and leaders of industry.

The 'Canadian Pacific' broke down before it arrived at Newport due to a wheel-bearing failure.

Mr Dean, a steam enthusiast, was slightly disappointed about the break-down but said: "At least it broke down before it arrived at Newport."

The event went as planned with a diesel train, the Fort William, pressed into service.

Newport mayor Ken Powell, one of the guests, said: "It was a very enjoyable day. There were no delays in the proceedings."

During the journey through Gwent and the Marches, in restored Pullman carriages, a raffle was held to raise funds for the Gwent Shrievalty Trust.

The Trust gives financial support to a number of projects aimed at helping communities.

First prize in the raffle, the steam

CHEERS TO MY YEAR: The High Sheriff of Gwent, Robin Dean, toasts his guests on the train hired to celebrate his year in office.
Inset left, the engine that was supposed to pull the High Sheriff's carriages and, inset right, the diesel engine which had to replace it

Picture:
MIKE
LEWIS

engine's headboard, was won by former prison governor Lyn Davies, of Llantrissent.

Summing up the day, another guest, Councillor Graham Powell, of Monmouthshire county council, said: "It was an excellently arranged visit to Shrewsbury.

"Our compliments go to the High Sheriff."

Above: Tea party at Qwaraguzi, Inyanga (*Left to right, standing*: Valerie Hanmer, Iona Shearer, Peta Pelletier, Douglas Leighton-Seager, Charles Hanmer; *seated* Hilary Wyrley Birch, Mrs Smith, Col. Wyrley Birch, Tessa O'Donnell). *(Page 16)*

I originally wanted to pack the boy back to Nyasaland as he is a bad lot but Mrs Susan W. Birch wouldn't hear of it. So it has come to a head now.

Lots of love

Robin

P.O. Inyanga
S.R.

14th October 1956

Dear Mummy

Your letter wasn't so late it only took a week arriving on the day that they usually come. I will give you all the details about clothing nearer to Christmas as the rainy season hasn't come on us yet. We are now in the hottest month of the year which is certainly not unbearably hot, most women are wearing summer frocks and men are in shirts.

This weekend I am at Qwaraguzi as Col and Mrs Wyrley Birch are away for a few days and I have been left in charge of the live-stock, pets etc., incidentally 12 dogs!

This week the local police are planning a big operation against cattle thefts as Col W. Birch and Bill Hanmer next door farmer have lost a lot between them all of which are unaccounted for. So the police in conjunction with the Portuguese police are making a large swoop on the border hills were there has been reported some mysterious lads roaming on the foothills.

On Friday I had to collect one of our most trustworthy African boys to go with the police for identifying the brands and earmarks. To find this boy I had to ride miles over the ranch searching every little hillock till I eventually found him. He is a full time hunting boy trapping down leopards and hyenas.

On Tuesday we are going down to the police station to listen in for a wireless report informing us how the operation is going on.

Whilst I was in the police station I found a map on the wall with red flags stuck in at various points; each flag represented a witch doctor!

During last week I have mainly been active in farming activities as now it is our spring and prior to the rains falling all the crops have to be sown and also I have been installing storm drains along the contour ridges. Erosion is the biggest menace to farms due to the heavy rain storms. 3 ins in an hour is not uncommon. During this week and until the rains we are mowing grass for bedding of feeding steers in the Kraals then making it into manure.

The little pet pig was auctioned at the church fete and he raised 19/6d, bought by a local inhabitant. The fete altogether raised £230 for the church organ. I didn't actually go but the young Wyrley Birches went.

During the week I visited the Rhodes Estate orchards growing apples, plums etc. The trees were very attractively laid out with rows of conifers acting as shelter belts. They had packing sheds for handling the fruit, the fruit boxes are made from locally grown trees. Also, on Rhodes Estate there are oak trees growing and now have just come into leaf making me quite homesick at the sight.

The other day it was my turn to collect the mail from the post office. I took the old model A Ford, when I came out of the post office a little old lady was admiring the car and she asked me "Where did you get that car from" and I replied "I think it originally came from Kenya". Then she said "it must have been mine then" and she had owned it for 21 years before the Wyrley Birches bought it. She was quite thrilled to see it again and had to be taken for a ride in it.

I am very grateful to you for giving a wedding present to Geoffrey and Caroline from us, you can deduct some money from my account to pay half share, incidentally Pop [nickname for my brother Martin] still owes me some money? We even heard here about exploits of debs and their escorts in the Rhodesian papers, so I am not surprised that the Mothers have toughened up especially that labour members have been raising protests in Parliament.

I am very amused about Lord Moynihan's son being sent off the Australia. His father hasn't a leg to stand on as he married second time a girl of 18 when he was in his fifties.

Lots of love

Robin

P.O. Inyanga

21st October 1956

Dear Mummy

Thank you very much for your last letter concerning the Hill Somerset wedding. I was very amused about the 'Rock and Roll' party in the basement. I haven't actually danced 'Rock and Roll' yet, but it has only just come to Salisbury. So I will make a point of seeing and hearing the new hit tune, especially after reading about Lord Moynihan's son in the Sunday paper under the heading of the Rock and Roll peer's son being warned by the police.

During the week I had a letter from Granny Head saying that she was very impressed with your flat and especially the bird pictures, she wrote to me from Woking.

I have now got a Land Rover. I finally ended up by buying a new one as I couldn't obtain a second hand one anywhere which was in good enough condition. Most buyers of Land Rovers out here seemed to keep them until they are completely worn out and also living up here I very rarely had the opportunity of going and inspective any second hand ones being 86 miles from Umtali and 150 miles from Salisbury.

The one I have has the same canvas top as Daddy's but it is much longer and roomier also; the seats are far more comfortable. I find driving it as comfortable as any car and it provides better comfort on these roads than many cars do.

I went to collect it on Thursday from the Umtali Rover agents. I managed to get a very reasonable comprehensive insurance from being a member of the A.A. which came to £11 and the tax for the year £10. Petrol here is only 3/- a gallon and some places 2/6d. The only item which is expensive is repairs; garages charge 22/6d an hour for labour for working on your car. This I hope will not apply to me as I will do all my own repairs of if any I hope. I am now carefully running in the engine for the next 1,000 miles.

I am not going to use the Land Rover in connection with my work as I have still got the use of the Ford. The main object of the purchasing of the car is for when you both come out in February and also I am seriously considering the overland trip back to England in 1957/58 as I wish to see Kenya, Nyasaland and the Congo. I am afraid I have inherited your love of travel. I am intending to go through to Kano, will Peter Gunning be there over those dates? I have christened the Land Rover "Rosalinda" from Schubert's ballet suite of that name.

This morning I went fishing for the first time on the lake, I caught a tiddler which I had to put back but nothing else as at the moment the weather is rather unsuitable. The lake is quite beautiful in spite of being artificial the setting might have been Scotland and this morning the lake was covered in attractive water birds. With the Land Rover I drove down to the water's edge much nearer than the other fishing folk who had to leave their cars on the road above. I will take father out on the streams and the lake in February. I got up at 4.30 am to get the morning rise as during the day it gets too hot and the fish don't move.

Col Wyrley Birch's daughter who farms at Marandellas is going to try and sell her milk through a shop in the town, she is going to bottle it into wax paper cartons with the metal clip. They asked me about the Tetra Pak machine as they saw an advertisement for it in a paper. I soon dissuaded them by the capital outlay on the plant as also it wouldn't work five minutes a day to pack their milk?

A Tetra Pak plant was offered to the farmers co op dairy in Salisbury, but they turned it down because they said it was cheaper to bottle their milk. I would like to hear John's opinion since he has been running the plant at Tattenhall.

I am glad you have another Twinkle this time, I hope not a shy breeder!

Lots of love

Robin

P.O. Inyanga

28th October 1956

Dear Mummy

I am writing this letter to you listening with great pleasure to 'La Traviata' on the radio. It is being broadcast in Afrikaans from S. Africa; they have some very good programmes. At the moment there is a music and drama festival at Johannesburg and 'La Scala' and Saddlers [sic] Wells have been out there. S. Africans are very cultural and appreciate good music especially the Dutch descendants i.e. Afrikanders.

During the week it has been very hot and sultry heralding the approaching rains and every afternoon clouds have been building up with thunder rumbling about in the heavens, in the evening dispersing again. Today it is very overcast with thunder; I feel it is going to rain. We certainly need it as the farm is very dry and we have to feed the cattle extensively. The only livestock seeming to benefit by no rain are the pigs. They are quite happy as long as they have a mud bath to wallow in when they get too hot. I have another 9 little ones this week bringing the total up to the hundred mark. I am now busy erecting new pig houses to accommodate the population.

Last Thursday I had to go and shoot two wild cows on Col Wyrley Birch's ranch. They had run berserk from the rest of the herd and we couldn't drive them to the slaughter poll. So, I had to carry out the execution on the Veldt. I drove to the area in an ex army truck like ours with the boys for skinning and cutting up of the carcases. After an hours searching I found the first cow and dropped her at 50 yards with a .303 service rifle. After being hit the cow just gently sunk on her knees and rolled over. The bullet went straight through the brain. Then I left the boys and went after the second and within half an hour I got her stone dead with my first shot. This time straight through the eye. I look upon this as being good practice for big game hunting at a later day.

This week I have been living with Anthony Wyrley Birch as his wife Susan is away in Salisbury for a month prior to expecting her baby. So we have been living a bachelor existence except that we have got a very good cook boy to cater for us.

During the week I caught two trout on the dam; they were good eating. Anthony got four also in the week. Uncle Geoff's rod is a great success and numerous people have asked me about it; the cost etc.

We had one excitement in the way of a car crash just outside the farm gates on a rather nasty bend. Two cars hit each other, one was rounding the bend on the wrong side of the road. The cars were both local one was owned by the manager of Rhodes Estate and the other the engineer of the roads department. Both were uninjured, the cars were badly damaged.

I am following the events in Hungary and Poland with great interest. I feel at last Russia has been getting some of her own medicine which she has been giving to us for the last 10 years in Malaya, Middle East etc.

On Saturday I made a very interesting trip in my Land Rover (Rosalinda) down to the Portuguese border to view some tea estates in the foot hills. The journey involved a drop of some 3,000 ft down a tortuous road switch-backing with at least a dozen hairpin bends. There was a drop of 800 ft on one side of the road. It is incredible how the country changes on this side. It was quite breath-takingly beautiful with the large mass of the mountain Inangani towering over the lush green valley with their rushing mountain streams crystal clear. Along the road I ran into the actual rain forest which was quite fascinating with the tall trees and creepers, tree ferns all growing in one tangled mass all thrusting their way sky wards in the great competition in obtaining light. The birds and butterflies were quite beautiful all exotic colours. The butterflies were large and fluttered about in the sunbeams coming through the treetops. The tea estates themselves are further down than I went as it meant a drive of 90 miles. I got as far as the offices and bungalows of the personnel. The buildings were all grouped around on the hills overlooking a lush green cultivated valley with nice sleek dairy cows grazing such a change after the dried up veldt around here.

On the way back to Inyanga I climbed to 7,800ft on the highest road in the Rhodesias and at that height the rarefied atmosphere has quite an effect on cars due to the lack of oxygen and also on the human body; I found it quite strain to climb on my feet at 8,000 ft. The Land Rover was also finding it an effort. I will certainly take you both down to the tea estates in February. I shall be interested to see how they compare with those you saw in Ceylon. I am making an itinerary of things I wish to show you when you come out.

During the week I had a letter from Pop all about his life in the Guards, complaining rather of hard work? And also one from Barbara, she says that she is fed up with Wincanton and bored so she is going to work in London next spring. I am glad she has taken the initiative at last to get away from her parents' grasp. I am very amused about Uncle Geoff's dilemma of the love lifes of the two Posnetts.

I wonder what will happen when Pop and myself get involved in a love affair let alone Victoria!

You must send me a photograph of Casey junior the pup.

Lots of love

Robin

PS. I am very sorry about Lady Curres death, the Wyrley Birches knew her.

P.O. Inyanga

4th November 1956

Dear Mummy

I enjoyed your letter on your description of the C.L.A. estate walk.

I used to enjoy Cirencester outings visiting estates and farms and the bus trip, sandwich lunches with bottles of beer. The great joy was watching the countryside slip by whilst you had a good view of the surrounding fields and farms with being higher than the hedges.

I was also very amused at the Raglans Farm walk and the pork and also our "Twink" in pup. I can hardly believe it after her indifference with her suitors.

This week I have been on my own as Anthony is in Salisbury visiting his wife prior to expecting her baby which is due very shortly. The biggest item of the week is that the rains have broken. We had the first last Sunday in a heavy thunder shower which took half an hour then two days break with thunder clouds building up then on the third night heavens really opened up. When I went to bed there was lightning and thunder rumbling in the hills around about. At 2.00 am it came, I was sleeping on the veranda and woke to the crashing crescendo of falling rain and thunder. It was like a bombardment in the days of trench warfare. The sky was lit up by continuous flickering and flashing of lightening nonstop without a pause, so it was almost clear as day. It was all sheet lightning no fork, gradually the intensity of the storm decreased and I was able to get some sleep. So ended my first impression of a tropical storm. Next day it rained all day with a steady downpour such as we experience on so many occasions in England. It might have been a wet day in Scotland with very overcast sky, cool with low clouds hiding the hills. It was lovely to hear the steady drip, drip of moisture falling from the trees and smell again the damp earth and foliage. It was the first real rain I have seen since leaving Cape Town.

It is amazing how the country changes after the rain, flowers seem to appear from nowhere. The air is full of sounds such as croaking of frogs, chirping of numerous crickets and birds singing. I must say there are some quite pleasant song birds. The African birds have their own characteristic songs attractive in their own way.

Night time is when Africa really wakes up as I sit writing my letters to you by the light of a paraffin lamp. The room is filled with myriads of insects, moths etc. all attracted by the light there are all shapes and sizes. Some look so weird that they might have come straight from prehistoric times. Some of the moths are quite beautiful with wing spans up to 6 inches. We get fire flies and glow-worms in hundreds. Along the streams and water courses it is like looking down on a town from the air with the numerous little lights.

There is also another inhabitant of the house which is always on the warpath after the insect life that is the house gecko lizard. His hunting grounds consist of the walls and the ceiling which he runs over with great agility, devouring the unsuspecting moth which gets in his pathway. His lair is somewhere in the thatch of the roof. Secret of running over walls and across the ceiling lies in his feet which are equipped with suckers.

During the week I had my first glimpse of a chameleon. I found it in the garden. It was a vivid green, but I picked it up and put it on my blue shirt, it objected strongly hissing like a locomotive rolling its eyes in a most uncanny fashion, one eye would be swivelled forward whilst the other would be watching the rear. It did turn a bluey green then I took pity on it and released it on a nearby tree. It clamoured up the branch where I placed it using its tail like a monkey's twining it around twigs. It had the most amazing feet adapted to climb trees.

I must say Africa has plenty of subjects for naturalists.

Lots of love

Robin

P.O. Inyanga

[No date]

Dear Mummy

I am sorry for you with Margaret away contending with all the chores etc. I hope she is better.

I am very pleased with the good news about Will. I always considered he was a very bold horse with plenty of courage. I hope you have a successful season point to pointing.

Well the great news here that the baby has arrived, it is a girl and Mrs W. Birch is thrilled as it is her first granddaughter after having three grandsons, also, I have been asked to be a god father which I have gladly accepted. Her name is Philippa. Now could you advise me on a Christening present? I can think of plenty of items for a small boy but not a girl.

On Tuesday I had to be called out of bed as Anthony's car broke a piston and he was stranded out in the wilds. He was just coming back from seeing Susan and the baby. Unfortunately, the engine of his car is quite beyond repair so had to leave the car on the roadside and transfer his luggage to mine.

Last Sunday I went with Col Wyrley Birch and visited one of the remote farms owned by an Afrikaans farmer, one of the early Dutch settlers. It was quite an amazing house built of burnt brick and finished with the bare minimum of furnishings only chairs and a table in the living room. The walls were adorned with family photographs of wedding groups etc.

But outside there were two new lorries and tractors and all sorts of machinery, all paid out of tobacco money. A lot of these farmers are incredibly well off but they always prefer to live their old ways. This farmer didn't even have a wireless and the first time he heard about the Middle East and Hungarian crises was when we told him about world events.

Most of these people are completely disinterested on what goes on outside their farms and families.

The Col wanted to do an exchange for some oxen with heifers. He suggested to buy the oxen but the Dutchman made him do a straight swop, so we picked 20 oxen out of his herd and the Dutchman at a later date picked 20 heifers matching in size to the oxen from the Col's herd. That is how they all do their business except when it comes to selling tobacco.

On Wednesday I went down to Umtali for to have the Land Rover serviced and also to buy Christmas cards. I am busy doing them this weekend. We have to dispatch them off this week to arrive in England in time for the 25th. It is a lovely drive down through the hills, the only thing marred it was that it rained some of the way and also I had a puncture but the garage found that the inner tube was faulty and replaced it free of charge. I must say that the front wheel drive of the Land Rover gives you great confidence on the slippery, muddy surfaces. I find Umtali the most attractive town and all the shops and business premises are very courteous and pleasant such a change after Newport – I shall certainly take you there in January.

It was very kind of Mrs Wyrley Birch to ask you to stay. I expect you will find it a very interesting and amusing experience like I have. I think it will fit in well like Mrs Bull's description of the Tints of Tint Hall in Ireland. As Qwaraguzi is overrun with dogs, animals etc. and the house is so typically English in character so unlike Rhodesian homes. It is furnished rather like Hinton with the little bric-a-brac miniatures and book shelves with dusty old volumes on the shelves, *Who's Who* etc.

I have sent Daddy a copy of the Royal show number of the Rhodesian farmer which he may find of interest. I wonder if you could send me the Dairy show number of the Farmer Stock Breeder and also the Smithfield one when it comes out. I am also enclosing a cutting about Tetra Pak from The Rhodesian farmer. There is interest being shown in it out here.

I have a stock exchange trip for Daddy that is Rhodesian Chartered Concession have found a large deposit of Pyrite ore.

Lots of love

Robin.

P.O. Inyanga

17th November 1956

Dear Mummy

We have been enjoying a week of wet English weather overcast, grey skies and cold. It is quite unbelievable considering the sun is directly overhead.

I have been castrating, worming and weaning the pigs this last week, 62 were weaned. I am very pleased how they have done. We have sold some as weaners to the local farmers around about as we haven't the room to fatten them.

During the week we had a near disaster as the herd boy lost four of our precious sheep being fattened ready for Christmas. He forgot to pen them up during the lunch hour. We searched for four consecutive days without luck and then they suddenly turned up, just wandered home. Most amazing considering how many wild animals abound the countryside.

We had also an appalling week for motor breakdowns and cars were abandoned over the roads by the Wyrley Birch family in the end Col Wyrley Birch went and bought a new Ford diesel lorry like our one, hoping it will solve the transport problems. I hope the lorry will be the answer as cars just won't stand up to the continual hammering on these bad roads.

I was interested to read in your last letter that John Rainforth is coming out here. I don't think there will be much hope in getting down the East coast with the canal blocked by the Egyptian sabotage. If he wishes to go home to Europe I would be delighted to take him but I don't propose to start until October 1957 as the Sahara route is closed through the northern summer months, open only from November to May.

I have made arrangements for a Christmas present for the family it is going to be in the nature of food stuffs. Everybody usually sends food parcels as consumer goods in the shops are just the same as in England and not much difference in price and if you buy anything overseas you get caught with purchase tax and at both ends custom duty.

I have got all my Christmas cards off. The shops are just beginning to get Christmas decorations but it isn't the same in the southern hemisphere seeing a Christmas tree with artificial snow whilst standing in blazing sunlight.

Next weekend I am going to stay with a friend of mine at a place called Gatoomia some 200 miles from here, so my letter may be a bit late. I am going via Salisbury will spend a night there and do some Christmas shopping.

Anthony has gone away again to Salisbury to fetch Susan and my god daughter Philippa, so I am running the concern on my own this week.

The Siamese kittens have grown up to the playful age they are very attractive but rather naughty. All the Wyrley Birches have got Siamese cats; they are quite intelligent but lack the character of old Poom our Silver Persian. They don't even steal! How is he keeping?

Anthony and I imported a chameleon into the house to keep down the insects. It is the most amusing creature, quite weird. I wish I could send one to Vicky. It has the most extraordinary habit of colour changing especially when annoyed it comes out in spots then stripes like a snake and puffs itself up to twice its size letting out hisses whilst I am writing this letter it is sitting on the lamp warming itself and striking out at any insect which comes within reach. The Africans are terrified of them. The cook boy wouldn't clean the room until we removed it. He was terribly upset when I handled it; he told me politely that I would quickly die from its bite. He is most amazed that I am still alive, assuming now that white men have some special magic.

Lots of love

From Robin

P.O. Inyanga
S.R.

25th November 1956

Dear Mummy

I am now writing to you from Salisbury. I am staying here for a couple of days Christmas shopping etc.

I left Inyanga on Friday and went down to a place called Hartley, where my friend Michael Lamb is working on a farm. It was a 300 mile trip along the main trunk road from Umtali via Salisbury to Bulawayo. A tarmac road right through.

The Land Rover cruised effortlessly at a steady 50 all the way and one stretch of 90 miles I didn't even change gear. The country I passed didn't vary much large tracts of bush which stretched for miles on end. Around Salisbury the bush had been mainly cleared and given over to farming. It is the first time I have been in the real farming district. It is most interesting as seeing these tremendous acreages of ploughed land up to 300 at a time without even a fence or any trees. Most of this land was planted down to maize and it was just coming up. Tobacco is done a smaller scale. Many times I passed gangs of Africans planting and hoeing.

This farm I stayed at was owned by one of the leading pig breeders of the country. The farm itself was terribly untidy, but the pigs were good except too much on the fat side and they had one or two which had gone off their legs and had to be hand fed! The herd was made up of landrace and large whites. They also had Jersey cows. Six hundred pigs altogether and three thousand poultry.

We visited several old goldmine workings as this is the heart of the gold mining district. I managed to find two good specimens of gold; one lying near the shaft head. I will have them valued at the Chamber of Mines tomorrow.

On Sunday Michael and I played golf at a course on the farm. I managed to beat him in spite that he led me around the first few holes but a thunder storm marred our play and we had to play darts in the 19th hole, i.e. the clubhouse.

Did I tell you that your photographs came, unfortunately the envelopes had burst so I hope they are all there. Certainly the caravan was a good size also I was interested in some of the photographs how the trees came down to the seashore. I wouldn't have thought it would be possible on the Atlantic shore with gales etc.

Tonight I am going to Salisbury to the latest "drive in cinema" where you have to sit in your car and watch the performance through the windscreen. The film title is Angles in Love with Ciceley Couteridge [sic] etc. Tomorrow I am going to the opening night of Reach for the Sky, story about Douglas Bader starring Kenneth Moore. I have been invited to join a party organised by a girl friend.

I hope all went well with Twink. I am awaiting your next letter for the results.

Tomorrow I am going to have an interview with the Chairman of the pig department in Rhodesian Cold Storage Commission to discuss the future of the pig industry and dairying. If I haven't sealed this letter by then I will write of my experiences.

Today I visited the AA offices here to make enquiries about motoring back through Africa. They were very helpful and I left the office with a large armful of notes. They said I should have no trouble at all with a Land Rover but do not recommend a normal car especially with the loads to carry and also I have to fit storage tanks to carry 30 gallons of petrol and 20 of water for the Sahara.

Lots of love

Robin

P.O. Inyanga

1st December 1956

Dear Mummy

I am terribly sorry about Carola's [Hopkinson] sudden death [from a tractor accident]. I always considered her a pleasant girl once away from the eyes of her parents. I agree with you about an evil influence on that house it is the second happening to that family within a year. I am very pleased that you sent a wreath.

I returned to Inyanga last Wednesday after a most enjoyable weekend. I had a talk with the Chairman of the pigs production division of the Cold Storage Commission of Rhodesia. It was most interesting 2 hours discussion about the future of pigs in the federation. He first told me that the pig industry in any country is always on a fluctuating market. But this country is well suited for pig production because of abundant cheap labour, cheap feeding stuffs and also the climate favours quick growth. And it is possible to turn a baconer out in six months instead of 8 months as in the cold temperate zones. The reason is that the pig requires the extra feed to keep itself warm as out here all feed is converted to flesh. Another point he made that one does not need such elaborate houses because of the warmer climate. I asked him about the future of landrace in this country, his answer was that they didn't have the stamina as the other breeds and he knew no-one who had any success out here.

On Tuesday I went on a trip to see my friend Michael Lamb's farm he had bought 50 miles from Salisbury. It was a pleasant drive through delightful countryside rather like Herefordshire with lush green valleys and the hills in the background such a contrast to south of Salisbury which is flat and featureless. I passed through some of the best farming country in the federation and also passed several gold mining townships. On this trip I had my first glimpse of really big indigenous trees. The road passed through great avenues of them making a most magnificent sight.

I visited Michael's farm which is about 800 acres. The farm was rather in a derelict state but the soil is very fertile and also benefits from being near a railway and main roads. On the roads I met with some of the worst mud I have seen yet in places the Land Rover was wading up to its axles. I have earmarked it as one of trips I will take you on. Altogether I covered about a thousand miles in the long weekend. The Land Rover went beautifully never using a drop of oil. The mark was the same on the dipstick as when I left Inyanga.

It must be awfully annoying for you having to cope with petrol rationing. Thank goodness we do not have to rely on the canal and our petrol is to be unaffected. All we have been told is that there may be a delay over certain imports.

Mrs Todd wrote to me from Johannesburg asking me down for Christmas, unfortunately, it will be impossible as Christmas is the busiest time for our firm, but I promised to go down at the end of January before Cousin Elizabeth goes home and also I want to tour the Union.

During the week I bought myself a very nice portable Pye wireless set for 10 gns at wholesale price as I got it through the butchery trading licence. It is incredibly cheap compared with U.K. prices as we have no purchase tax on them.

I had a letter from Granny Head it was full of warning things that I mustn't do such as climbing up to 8,000 feet. You had better not tell her that I plan to go 19,000 feet next year on Africa's highest mountain! She tells me the height will be bad for my heart.

Lots of love

Robin

P.O. Inyanga

5th December 1956

Dear Mummy

Thank you for your London letter. I am sorry that our sheep were beaten but I suppose that the law of averages won't allow a success every time!

I was surprised to see that John is planning to come out here with you. I hope he can come as I am sure he will be very interested in this county.

I am delighted that Daddy has been elected to the R.A.S.E. and I am sure that "Squeaky" Price [the losing candidate] must have been most offended.

On Tuesday I went down to Umtali to have my Land Rover serviced. I certainly had my most muddy motoring experience as the road down was in a terrible state after repeated rain on it. There were lorries and cars abandoned all down the route. The Land Rover took it all in its stride wading through the mud. When I got to the garage the mechanic had to hose it down before commencing work on it.

I spend the day in Umtali buying various ingredients for Christmas cakes, puddings etc. to be made by Mrs Wyrley Birch Sen. and Susan. After lunch whilst drinking my coffee on a hotel veranda I was overhearing annual general meeting of a firm and as the meeting closed there was much clapping for the chairman congratulating him on a good financial year's trading and then all the directors filed out. I have never seen such a sight, all dressed in double breasted suits carrying a brief case and the report of the finances. The best part was everyone had a tremendous girth around the middle. They all stood in groups on the veranda talking then one by one departed climbing into their large American sedans and Jaguars. I later found out the reason for the large girth around the middle was due to the firm in question dealt in confectionery!

Some news has just reached my ears that the Umtali motor bus which runs up to here has had a bad smash and 35 Africans have been injured. It skidded and went over a bridge parapet landing in a river. This bus carries all our meat orders so we will have to make them up again depending how much has been spoilt.

Tomorrow we have a Gymkhana here and at the moment the farm is overflowing with horses as the farm is near the show ground so all the riding folk have deposited their horses for the night with us and I am wondering how many will be there in the morning?

In the events I have been asked to ride so I will tell you about it next week.

I must thank Vicky for her very original present in the shape of a Model A Ford kit. I have made it up and it has turned out very well. I must say Vicky thinks up the most original ideas.

Unfortunately, the old Ford here is off the road with back axle trouble. It was scheduled to take the Father Christmas to the Inyanga children's party but Father Christmas had to go by the next oldest car in the district.

Lots of love

Robin

PS. I hope the pups are doing well.

P.O. Inyanga

8th December 1956

Dear Mummy

I am delighted that all went well with Twinkle and the pups are doing well. Are you planning to keep some or sell? I should think you would find a very easy market. I would love a photograph of the family group if you could get Daddy to undertake it one day before they go.

I am sorry about no hunting I must say Canadian pox is a new one on me in animal diseases.

I am also very surprised to read in your letter that Barbara wishes to come out here. If Barbara comes out I would suggest to work in Salisbury or any other centre. Secretaries are very much sort after. I wouldn't suggest a farm as she may find it very isolated and to my knowledge there are a very few farmers who are well off enough to employ a full time secretary. The only people who do are Land development companies or Estates. In Salisbury itself there is good social life and sports clubs etc.

I myself will be leaving here after you have departed and I intend to live within the Salisbury area as out here in Inyanga it is very isolated and also I want to find a job with more scope than I get here. The main reason I stayed on is to help Anthony whilst he had to be away a lot during the last two months.

You also mentioned about the Wyrley Birches' relative named Learoyd. He is out here and he used to work for Vivien Bishop in Herefordshire. His home is Cheltenham. I met him on one occasion; he came and stayed the weekend at Qwaraguzi.

Last Wednesday I went to the Inyanga districts Old Servicemen's dinner held in honour for those who served in both world wars. It was mainly supported by ex Indian Army. We had a slap up dinner followed by many speeches and back slapping. Then a film show where I think practically everybody fell asleep during the performance!

Disaster struck next day as most of Inyanga went down with food poisoning including myself who was a good bit luckier than the rest, I escaped lightly only missing the morning's work. Some were very ill, it was tracked down to the pork we had at dinner.

We had just got a new doctor and this was his first introduction to Inyanga. He is a very nice person and he is very keen on photography and possesses a lovely new Leica camera which cost £285 with all the equipment. He was quite enthusiastic about my photographs.

I was horrified to learn that petrol had gone up to 6/- (six shillings) a gallon in the UK, it is now twice the price that it is here. I see you will be all on 'Vespa scooters'.

I had my Land Rover serviced and also finished off my Christmas shopping. We have a few Christmas parties up here in the Christmas week.

The weather has been just like typically English summers overcast with numerous showers. The hills look most attractive shrouded in mist with just the peaks thrusting their way through.

I am now listening to one of my favourite Beethoven symphonies on my new portable radio. I am very satisfied with it especially with the tone.

I can hardly believe it is so near Christmas the only signs are that a few Christmas cards are coming through the post.

Lots of love

From Robin

P.O. Inyanga

16th December 1956

Dear Mummy

I am replying to your letter about your trip. Could you tell me if your plane lands at Livingstone as it would be best for you to visit the Victoria Falls from there otherwise if you come straight to Salisbury you would have to double back on your tracks to visit the falls?

I propose to meet you at Livingstone either with the Land Rover and then motor back to Salisbury visiting places of interest on the way or I would fly to the falls from Salisbury then back with you. I should suggest a two day stay at the falls; the hotel is one of the best in Africa, then move on to Salisbury for another two day stay. So you can do a bit of shopping and sightseeing etc. before going on to Inyanga.

It will be a bit of a problem about John as I don't think I can arrange any accommodation for him. I would suggest Anthony W. Birch as he is John's contemporary in age but he has only a small cottage and with two children, another point that the Land Rover will only seat three comfortably and riding in the back is rather uncomfortable on these bad roads.

Aunt Betty P wrote saying she is coming as well so I plan that she and John ought to go down to the Union from Salisbury where we can meet them later.

Can you let me know fairly soon what you would like to do over the falls visit as will go ahead with hotel reservations etc. I expect you will stay in Salisbury with friends of the W. Birches' for the two days.

I do not want you to bring anything thank you but I would like you to take an overcoat back to England as I find no use for it here.

Also, could you bring me out £50 in travellers cheques for my proposed tour of the Union.

I will give you the local news in my next letter.

Love, Robin

P.O. Inyanga

7th Jan 1957

Dear Mummy

Thank you very much for your two letters. I am afraid I have got behind hand with my letter writing as I have been away for the weekend, which I will tell you about later in this letter.

We had a wonderful New Year's party full of gusto. A party again just like one of the Llangibby dances, paper hats and false noses and lots of rowdy dances etc. It was all the greatest of fun. I finally toddled off to bed in the early hours of the morning. The other party I had was at the Hanmers where we had to set off in one of the worst thunder storms of the season. The time I got to the party my Land Rover was crammed with people who I picked up on the way when their cars got stuck on various hills. The party was one of those which started off as a cocktail party then it developed into playing 'charades' and other games of that nature and finally ending up with dancing. The Hanmers have a very nice house and the farm the biggest in the district.

This weekend I went on a trip to a place called Mount Selinda some 200 miles south of Umtali. I have always wanted to see that country as it is part of the border mountain chain which stretches down eastern border of the federation. The first night I stayed in Umtali and then the next day I motored through the most lovely country with the road winding in and out of the hills. This is certainly the best country I have seen yet in Rhodesia. It beats Inyanga in spite of Inyanga having the higher mountains but Inyanga

88

is bleak like Scotland as this Melsetta district, as it is known, is far greener with more trees very like the borders of Wales.

The reason it is greener as it is much nearer to the sea thus getting a more temperate climate. The mountains were quite rugged very like Snowdonia. They are known as the Alps of Rhodesia. This area is also a large forestry area and I passed many plantations of pines and wattles trees. The forestry commission are building a magnificent new road which was a pleasure to motor on.

The place where I stayed at called Mount Selinda is unique as on top of this mountain is the last of the primeval forest which stretched over Rhodesia. There is only 3,000 acres left. It was a wonderful experience driving and walking under the great mahogany trees, some up to 100 ft high all festooned in creepers and other parasites. Walking through the forest was quite an uncanny experience it was dark, gloomy and silent except the drip, drip of moisture and the chatter of birds high up above in branches. Walking along the paths reminded me very much of the Arboretum at Westonbirt. Just outside the forest in a clearing there was an American mission station, one of the oldest in the country, established 1893. I must say it was beautifully laid out with very fine buildings.

I stayed on a tea estate just at the foot of the mountain right on the border of Portuguese territory. I arrived at the tea estate to look up a friend of the Wyrley Birches, but I discovered that he had been moved off to another estate. The manager hearing of this asked me to stay for the weekend at his house, (Rhodesian hospitality!) which I did. He had a delightful family and was an ex Assam planter so I had a real Indian weekend, mangos for breakfast, curry for lunch and then drinks on the bungalow veranda watching the sun go down. I had a wonderful tour of the estate and the factory which was most interesting. It was a 3,000 acre estate. The manager and his wife were great music fanciers and I had great pleasure in listening to my favourite Beethoven and other lovely records.

Mt Selinda is the furthest point south of the mountain chain and from the bungalow you could see just a few small foothills then absolutely flat plain stretching as far as the eye could see into the Transvaal south and Portuguese territory east.

On Monday I returned back the short route to Umtali transversing low country along the foothills, the temperature was up in the 90's most of the way and I was in some places only 1500 feet above sea level.

I stopped for a short break at a place called hot springs where I saw the spring in question bubbling up, the water was quite hot and smelt of bad eggs! Quite a number of people bathe in it for health reasons.

I arrived back at Inyanga in the usual rain storm.

The Land Rover went beautifully proving itself to be just as happy cruising at 50 on the good main roads or transversing rough secondary roads.

I am off to Salisbury today with Col Wyrley Birch to make arrangements for your trip to the falls and other places I have in mind for you.

This I expect will be my last letter to you before seeing you next week. I shall meet you at the airport with car at 2.40 on the 16th. I am very much looking forward to seeing you again.

With lots of love

Robin

Durban

20th February

Dear Mummy

As you will see that my progress has brought me as far as Durban. I won't tell you about Johannesburg or Stegi Swaziland as I expect you have heard about it all from Daddy.

After leaving the family on route for the Kruger game reserve I set sail for the Drakensburg Mountains where I spent a most enjoyable weekend climbing and I climbed a 9,000 ft peak. The highest ones went over 10,000 ft. The mountains themselves were most majestic. I stayed at a guest farm in the foothills. After leaving the Drakensburgs I motored onto Mooi river where I visited a friend of the Wyrley Birches. She was a cousin of Pop's house master T.A. Brocklebank. She told me that he taught French by the use of a dictionary and only got to Eton through his rowing achievements, just what Pop told me. At Mooi river I stayed with Count and Countess Jankowich they were both Hungarian refugees who left Hungary before the Russians took over after the last war. They have a lovely farm in Natal and a house in Durban. I spent a couple of days on the farm.

Natal is certainly one of the nicest parts of the Union I have seen yet. This farm was mainly dairy and pigs. Also, Merino sheep and some fat stock.

The most unique part of the farm was all the fencing was done by stone walls so it looked just like the Cotswold Country as it was all rolling downs.

Natal is the most English part of South Africa and parts of it is so typical English winding roads passing through villages and even country mansions with lodge gates and tree lined avenues. What impressed me most was the freshness of the countryside and the general prosperity and flourishing of everything.

The Count and Countess had some of those lovely Lipizzaner horses which are used at the Spanish Riding School Vienna. They managed to get four out before the occupation, now they have got a good stud. They had some in training for dressage at Johannesburg.

The Count and Countess are the most charming people and they are both great music lovers, so I have been in my element. They have got a family of seven but only two girls are here at present, the rest are scattered over Africa some are at the moment helping the refugees in settling and finding jobs here. There are two daughters living here at the moment one of Victoria's age and the other 19. So my stay in Durban has been a round of fun. I am staying in a very nice house overlooking the sea and harbour. This house is one of the older ones dating from the Edwardian days. In my round of parties I have visited some most magnificent houses in the suburbs, air-conditioned with swimming pools etc.

The great excitement here at the moment is that we have the Coronia in harbour with the Americans on board with the world cruise costing £1,000 a piece.

The other night I went with the Count and Countess and had dinner at the American Consulate and we met some of the passengers. They were a typical middle age lot mostly taking the cruise just after the husbands had retired from a profession or business.

The tours were run on the typical American lines everything seen in the minimum of time, most of them had left the ship at the Cape and flown in land to see the sights of Africa then to join the ship again here before going on to India were they will leave the ship at Bombay and see India in a week before joining the Coronia again at Colombo.

The pace was too much for one old girl and she got mixed up whether Durban was in India or not? She thought her fellow passengers were pulling her leg when they kept on telling her that it was still Africa. She told us that she was convinced it was India by seeing so many Indians on the quay side when the Coronia docked. I must say one sees more Indians here than Africans and most of them very prosperous driving around in large American cars with big families.

Durban is really tropical, hot and humid with hot nights but there are sea breezes which are very pleasant. I must say it was lovely to see the sea again. The sea front is very attractive but very like any other part of the world with ocean view hotels and amusement parks. The Countess took me to the snake park where we examined the numerous varieties of snakes, lizards etc.

I hope you both had a good journey home again in the Britannia did the Wyrley Birches see you off at Salisbury?

The Land Rover is going very well and I have completed 3,000 miles since seeing you last in Salisbury at the cost of only £15 and the only repair I had to do is to replace the fan belt.

My next stage is the 1,100 miles to Cape Town where I hope I can give you a permanent address.

Cheerio for the present.

Lots of love

Robin

Dear Mummy

I am giving you a progress report of my travels down the coast
from Durban, altogether 1,300 miles from here. It was a most interesting trip as I passed through four separate climatic zones from
the sub tropical region around Durban, through desert in the Karroo,
Mediterranean climate and the most southern tip of Africa which
has the same type of climate as England, rain all the year round
then back to Mediterranean climate of the Cape.

The journey from Durban to East London was most interesting;
first I passed through Zululand which was mostly African reserves,
then the Transkei again mostly African reserves. The Africans there
are far more attractive than the ones of Rhodesia as they still dressed
in their traditional costumes and also they rode the Basuto ponies.
I saw more Africans on ponies and horses than I did on bicycles.
The country was mostly rolling grassland not very much bush and
the native villages were most attractive, neat round huts all white-
washed. I have taken many photographs.

The drive between East London and Port Elizabeth was mainly
through rather dry country and very little farming activity. But, from
Port Elizabeth to a place called Knysna was quite beautiful as this
area has rain all the year around and the country was mountainous
with mountains coming down to the sea as on the North Wales
coast.

The road made its way through huge forests such as we saw at

Mount Selinda. There trees weren't actually the same species but similar in appearance, every so often the road dipped down to the sea shore past lovely sandy beaches and coves as on the Devonshire coast. I spent a weekend at Knysna in the heart of the district, from here I drove inland to visit the ostrich farming district of Oudtshoorn. It was one of the most interesting drives I have done as I drove up from Knysna on the coast through large tracts of forest and mountains. Once I was over the mountain pass the country completely changed as I entered the desert of the little Karroo, one side of the mountains were lush and green and then the complete contrast. The ostrich industry is not what it used to be but I saw a good number in fields just the same way as cattle are kept.

From Knysna I went on to Cape Town. I must say it was lovely to see the Table Mountain again; the country was very much browner than it was when I was last here because now it is the dry season being in the winter rainfall area.

There is great activity at the moment as the grapes are ripening so is the fruit. The first day in Cape Town I spent the day looking up old acquaintances many being surprised to see me.

The Land Rover went beautifully and gave no trouble at all in the entire trip.

Lots of love

Robin

Kings Kloof
Somerset West
Cape Province

28th February 1957

Dear Mummy

I have just paid a visit to Aunt Betty Posnett who's staying here a week before sailing and I was very upset to hear from her that Granny isn't at all well, Aunt Betty was very worried whether she should fly home or not but we were very thankful when we got a cable from Aunt Marjorie stating that Granny was better. I stayed at their hotel for the Posnett's last night and I took Elizabeth out to a party to meet some of my Cape Town friends on her last night.

Whilst I have been here I have been job hunting with the very kind assistance of Col Newton King who was in the war with Col Wyrley Birch. Col Newton King has a fruit farm here. I have been very attracted by the fruit farming especially grapes. I am happy to get on a fruit farm or a mixed farm.

I went for an interview with a farmer near here who was one of the leading Jersey breeders but he couldn't take me on as he wanted somebody for at least two years to take the place of his son who is in England. He had a lovely farm very neat and orderly it was in the grain growing belt. I have another interview tomorrow.

If I am not successful I will have to make my way north again otherwise money will run short.

Somerset West is very much the place where the army and civil servants retire, the town is beautiful situated between mountain of 5,000 ft and the sea; all round are vineyards and orchards. Col Newton King took me over a big estate which had a turnover of

¼ million a year in fruit, and had its own canning factory and forestry to make the fruit boxes.

Cape Town docks are very active because of the Suez Canal blockage and every night the bay is full of ships waiting to dock. I have counted up to 20 waiting to come in.

Aunt Betty gave me your letter which she picked up at Johannesburg. I was very glad you enjoyed yourself at the Bells. I was very amused at your description of the trip to Zimbabwe ruins in the Rolls. John and I didn't go as it was an all day trip to Beit Bridge. I am glad that the Wyrley Birches came to see you off. When I am next in Rhodesia I will give you a report on how the Bell's house is progressing and the plumbing?

I have been enjoying the wonderful sea bathing down here, great fun surfing in the big Cape rollers.

Down here is just like living in Europe as there is a dense population per square mile and all the farms are in European units. 100, 300 acres etc. The country in parts is very like Scotland to look at even to real heather other parts more like the Cotswolds in the open growing area. All the corn has been cut and they are now sowing for the next season. Wheat grows through the winter as there is no frost.

I have completely fallen in love with the Cape it has got everything even to a pack of fox hounds of which I have heard very amusing stories. Somewhat run on the Llangibby lines. It hunts jackal or failing that it becomes a drag hunt.

I have been quite impressed with South Africa as a whole but the standard of living is not anything like as high as Rhodesia and some of the white farmers live in a very peasant like way with small arid farms and often you see them riding in donkey carts as in Ireland. Most of those farmers are descended from the Dutch Boers.

Here the cost of living is very much lower. I had my car serviced here in Cape Town and it was done at half the cost of the Salisbury garages equivalent. At the moment what upsets all the English people is the present government but everyone is fairly confident for the future election.

One thing I have noticed here is that we get a long summers day nearly two hours difference than Rhodesian days. The rains start again in April at the moment the weather is blissful. I am amazed at the locals who are complaining of the heat it is nothing like as warm as Rhodesia and also we get a cool breeze blowing from the sea.

Cape Town is full of Rhodesians on holiday and when I pass a Rhodesian car there is much horn blowing and hand waving. On the way down I always had the passenger seats filled with hitch hikers. One stage I had a party of South African army cadets who were dropped out in the country on an exercise but when I asked them to help me find a road on the map I found that none could read a map and pointed in opposite direction.

My address is: c/o Col. Newton King, Kings Kloof, Somerset West, Cape Province.

Lots of love

Robin

PS. I do hope Granny is better.

Cape Town

9th March 1957

Dear Mummy

So far I haven't been successful in finding the right sort of job as in this country one has to be brilliant in knowing Afrikaans the language of the Dutch settlers. That has been my stumbling block as everyone seems to require it here and also I have been very much put off by the present Nationalistic government.

The Cape to my mind is a most lovely place to live but has been utterly spoilt by the hatred between the three races; English, Dutch and the Africans, all at each other's throats. I have spent most of the week going around visiting farms etc. some of which I found very interesting. It is amazing what they had achieved on a poor stony soil.

On Tuesday I visited the Cape Town show. I was rather disappointed by it as it wasn't nearly as good as the Salisbury show. All the stands were badly laid out, no amenities which one appreciates at shows, and also, what struck me was the appalling dirt everywhere in the form of waste paper etc. Everyone considers the British public untidy but the Afrikaners are much worse. I went on the second day and it could have easily been the last due to the paper scattered about everywhere.

At the show I met a great friend of mine who was at Cirencester with me. He had just come back from Canada and was on his way up to Rhodesia where his parents live.

He and I watched the ring events which were quite good especially the horses. The Dutch farmers are very fond of horses and mules and resulting the show had some very fine turnouts. The most interesting class was the judging of the mule teams where they had spans up to 8 in harness pulling a four wheel wagon. At one stage they went around the ring at a full gallop and the drivers controlled them with a long raw hide whip which he cracked in the air above the mules' heads.

The funniest event was when the mules and brood mares were being led around the ring. One mule bolted with its African boy groom. He vainly held on until he tripped and was pulled along the ground for a hundred yards till his trousers came off all buttons being severed. Everyone was splitting their sides with laughter. I must say he was in a very difficult predicament one hand holding the mule the other his trousers and wondering what he should let go of first, trousers or mule.

You may have seen in your papers that the Archbishop of Cape Town has died from a heart attack. I gather from local resources that he was quite a character and was the mainstay of the Anglican church of South Africa in its fight against the present government "Apartheid Bill" which is coming in force to separate Africans from whites in all public meeting places.

I should address your next letter to the Todds at Blandford where I will stop on the way north. I wish Daddy a Happy Birthday.

Lots of love

Robin

Dear Mummy

I am now staying with the other Wyrley Birches who have a farm here. I came up from Cape Town last Tuesday which is a 500 mile trip. I averaged 50 mph from Cape Town to here in the Land Rover. The road on which I came was the finest I have ever travelled on. The country was all desert as I passed through the Karroo desert.

The farm here is in semi desert country and is the centre for the race horse breeders and sheep farmers. This family of Wyrley Birches is quite different from the Inyanga ones. George W. Birch is an old Etonian and has married a South African wife; they also have a large family and are Catholics. There house is very nice and large, the furniture is from the old family home in Norfolk and the family portraits adorn the walls.

The country around is just like what one sees in the American wild western films. I must say in spite of the semi desert this is to my mind one of the richest farming areas in South Africa and they keep merinos here.

On Wednesday I went to the local show at Colesburg. I was very impressed with it. Most of the farmers are Afrikanders but they are all of a good type and very well off thus being not to politically minded. These Afrikanders are very keen on horses so the turnout was very good at the show. We also had a demonstration of rough riding and breaking in of horses all very much in the wild western style.

The Wyrley Birches have the Orange River flowing along one boundary of their farm so they have got a good irrigation scheme along the banks for growing lucerne which is cut as hay for the horses and sheep.

George Wyrley Birch is not all like the Col. To my mind rather like Uncle Pat in the manner of speaking and looks. He was in the last war but was taken prisoner early on in the desert. He has the same failing as the Col. In that is he is a great talker and story teller!

There is one son at home aged 24 and he and I go round together on the farm doing jobs with sheep etc. We are shortly going to embark on shearing 800 merinos. The sheep farms are modelled on the Australian lines and when shearing comes round everyone has a large team to shear which travels the district.

The Wyrley Birches have a railway siding on the farm which is a great asset and also we get a paper and post every day.

On Friday evening John W. Birch and I went fishing in the Orange River and I managed to hook a large type of carp which I successfully landed without much of a struggle.

The climate is blissful, sun shining every day, not too hot as we are at 4,000 ft. The air is like wine, everyone says that this is one of the healthiest spot in the world. The rainfall is 15 inches a year and lies in the summer rainfall area.

The characteristic sight here is the numerous windmills for pumping as all water is from boreholes. The water is very hard due to the high lime content. The livestock here has made the district famous for its racehorses.

Colesburg was a centre for squirmishes during the Boer war and I have been shown many relics, such as old block houses, grave yards etc. The Wyrley Birches have also a large collection of munitions which have been found on the farm.

Did you go to the Gold Cup meeting at Cheltenham? The results were printed on our local papers.

Has Will had his first outing yet? George W. Birch has just interrupted my letter writing in showing me some of his photographs of horses he has bred.

Yesterday we had a tennis party for the benefit of me meeting the locals, every farm has its tennis courts thus the standard is very good. These sheep farmers live a very good life and after lunch everyone goes and has a snooze. I went into my room just after lunch and found a guest stretched out my bed snoring!

I think it will be safer if you send my next letter to the Todds at Blandford as I will be moving on about the middle of next week.

Cheerio until next Sunday.

Lots of love

Robin

16th April 1957

Dear Mummy

I am staying the weekend with the Bells. I have been up to Inyanga for the week to see the Wyrley Birches. They are all very well and to my surprise they have now got a Land Rover a long wheel base model. She bought it but is now exclusively used by the Col and Mrs Wyrley Birch has to be contented with the old Ford! They said they were so impressed how my one went so they took the plunge.

The weather is quite wonderful as this is the best time of the year here. At Inyanga the nights were quite frosty and the mornings just like our English Septembers, crisp and clear.

There has been further alterations in my plans as Anthony wants me to take over the butchery for a month as he and Susan are going on holiday, so I will do that starting after Easter and then at the end of May or the beginning of June I will return home for the summer and I will apply in England for a job as an overseas rep for Africa which I mentioned in my last letter.

The Bells have very kindly offered to lay up my Land Rover on their farm and also store my belongings here which will be very convenient being so near Salisbury.

Certainly Peter Thorneycroft gave you all a very attractive budget. I imagine you will now extend your racing activities with less entertainment tax.

Whilst I was at Inyanga I met David Stirling [of the SAS fame 'Who Dares Wins'] who is an important figure in the Capricorn

Africa Society which you may have read about in the English papers.

It was wonderful to be back at Qwaraguzi almost as good as returning to Glen Usk. Naturally nothing had changed except that there were some more litters of kittens and puppies. Young Nigel and Anthony's dog Laura gave me a great welcome. The only people I met were the Hanmers and Pearces; both asked after you all.

Yesterday the Bells and myself went motor racing at Salisbury. It was a most entertaining day several British drivers were competing.

I am spending Easter with Pat and John Mclewaine at Larkhill. They have asked me to play polo cross with them which will be fun.

At the moment I am staying with the Malcolmes in the Bells' old house, sleeping in the room with the bees. I think you also slept there. The Malcolmes have been very kind in providing early morning tea. They are certainly a very nice couple.

We are still getting rain here, very unusual for this time of year and it was very wet at Inyanga. No more Hyena troubles or Leopards. The sheep are lambing again – a good crop so far.

Lots of love

Robin

PS. The Bells send their regards.

c/o Barclays Bank
Salisbury

23rd April 1957

Dear Mummy

I received the first of your letters at my new address last week. I am sorry that poor Will had not a very successful first outing but I am awaiting anxiously for your next letter to see how he fared at the Glamorgan point to point.

I am not surprised about the Vespa's wheel coming off as I had previously warned Margaret to check it at least once a week as it was pointed out in the instruction book. I think if you can keep the Vespa going till I come back and I will buy her a light weight motor cycle such as a BSA Bantam or a Francis Barnett. They are much more robust than any of the motor scooters. You also mentioned the Parella which Arthur Alsop stocks but I consider Margaret lives too far away, so I imagine it would never be serviced.

I have booked to come home the first week of June but the date hasn't been confirmed yet. I have chosen a Viscount service not Britannia as I have heard everybody has complained about the seating discomforts etc.

I will be going up to Inyanga at the end of the month to take over the butchery for Anthony.

At the moment I am building a garage at Swallowfield for laying up the Land Rover whilst I am in England.

We have had a wintery Easter with cold winds, but it was sunny the first of the cold snaps. I expect I told you in my last letter that I was spending Easter at Larkhill.

Last Saturday I was introduced into the game of polocrosse, I played in several chukkas.

The first one I played back and didn't have very much to do as my side was on the attack, the second I played up in the forwards and was kept very busy. The pony I was riding was called Slipstream; I rode it when I stayed there. She is marvellous and follows the ball in an uncanny way. By the time I had played several times and had some practice I became quite proficient at catching the ball on the move.

I was congratulated on my play by the members of the club – for a beginner. I am fortunate that I have been schooled on the horsemanship side so it is just a question of getting my eye in and making shots. It will be a sport which I will take up when if I am settled in the country from this one graduates onto polo.

We all went to polo on Easter Sunday at a place called Bromley and John Mclewaine was playing. The polo was fairly good about the same standards as the 2nd teams at Cirencester Park. They had a very nice ground with a club house etc.

The Wheelers were also staying for Easter and they asked to be remembered to you. Mrs Wheeler who you didn't meet was very nice. She is John's sister.

Timmy and Roy were both very well and surrounded by Easter eggs. Katherine was spending her holiday here riding and schooling horses for the forthcoming shows.

I was very surprised to read in your last letter that Cousin Jennifer Johnson was engaged to Tim Dobell!

I am also rather amused that John is taking an interest in Helen Robinson there was correspondence being exchanged when John was out here. I think that Helen has some connection with the Murray-Ushers. I can't remember anything special about Helen except that she is the large and homely type!

Certainly the Cheshire Mothers will be kept very busy with wedding arrangements in the forthcoming year.

Everybody here is waiting anxiously for the results of Welensky's talks in London.

Lots of love

Robin

29th April 1957

Dear Mummy

I am highly delighted to hear that Will won his race at Glamorgan it must have been very exciting for you all. He certainly must have had good odds. I hope this will be one of many successes. He certainly may be a promising steeplechaser. I will await eagerly for your next letter after Berkerley pt to pt.

I am sorry that you haven't received a letter from me for some time but I have dispatched one regularly every week since being back here so it must have gone astray or delayed.

Did you all go to Badminton? I have been following it from the BBC overseas news.

The great excitement here is the return of Sir Roy Welensky as Prime Minister. I think that some of the government is somewhat disappointed that there wasn't more concessions granted but I consider a gradual change over to Dominion status is a better thing in the long run.

One of your letters which has just caught up with me and you mentioned about a job in Tasmania. I wonder if you could give me details as I am very interested, as much as I love this country and its people I have always had a hankering after Tasmania as you will know.

I have still an open mind and I haven't committed myself to anything yet. At the moments I consider a farming proposition is out of the question here due to the present structure of the agriculture markets and prices. This year there has been another surplus of maize and the government has been exporting it at a loss of £1 a bag. The only enterprise worth considering is tobacco but it requires such a large capital outlay with rather too much of a risk attached to the growing side so many people have gone bust due to crop failures.

For running a business in town there is the problem such as small markets with a high cost of transport etc. and also the very overrated values of town property.

With my year here I have got a very good idea of conditions. I have come to the conclusion that the only real advantage of living here is saving in income tax and having servants, which to my mind are essential as one very shortly kills oneself doing the chores with our climate as well as the height to contend with. The cost of living is about the same as England, some things here are cheaper but others are more costly so it eventually evens out.

I have met several people out here who have been to Tasmania saying it such a lovely place with a delightful climate much warmer winters than England but otherwise much the same.

With my visit to the sheep farms in the Karroo of South Africa I have been rather taken with sheep breeding and Tasmania is the centre of breeding Merino stud rams for the mainland. Also, mixed farming is practiced on the same lines as in England.

I also gather there is hunting but I don't know what they hunt, I suspect kangaroos or wallaby. Unfortunately here it is not very practical, and on top of the effort of keeping a horse with horse sickness etc.

One thing that I rather doubt there will be in Tasmania is the wonderful generosity and friendliness of the Rhodesians as I imagine most Tasmanians will have little in common with the English as they will be probably in their third and fourth generations, but I can't really say until I have been there.

If I leave here for an indefinite period the Bells have offered to buy my Land Rover from me as the Rolls now cannot be taken off the tarred roads because of its age and costly repairs. I shall be very sad to part with it as it has been such a faithful, trusty servant, unless Father would like it for the farm as it's being a more recent model than his present one. I could bring it back by sea.

I will let you know when I am going up to Inyanga. I am at present awaiting a letter from Anthony stating when he wants to leave for his holiday.

I am sorry that Granny hasn't been well again but I hope she soon recovers.

Lots of love

Robin

Aftermath

I think looking back it was due to parental concerns that I was persuaded to return to the United Kingdom. My father especially requested my help with the running of the family farm which had grown somewhat in size by taking in hand additional land. Also, as the eldest son, I would be required to take up my responsibilities especially now that my father was getting on in years. Sadly he was to die at a relatively young age of sixty six from cancer of the throat, ten years after my return.

I decided to fly back to England on one of the newly introduced BOAC Viscounts, a turbo prop aircraft powered by two Rolls Royce "Dart" engines. From my seat looking out to the port engine the word Rolls Royce gave me great assurance with the familiar RR badge attached to the engine cowling. The very reassuring whistling of the turbo prop engines made the flight so relaxing, via stop overs at Entebbe, Benghazi, Rome, and finally London.

Looking back I now feel rather ashamed: what I did was to conceal a chameleon in my hand luggage. These admirable lizards with their ability to change colour according to their background became quite a pet to which I had a strong attachment.

On my return home I released it in our greenhouse where it was perfectly happy on its diet of European flies and created much interest in my family and friends, but sadly after more than a month in captivity it escaped and afterwards was never seen again.

After my time in Rhodesia I did find Britain rather insular or suburban and it took a little while for me to adjust myself to a different lifestyle after the wide open spaces of Africa, with its challenges and unpredictable climate. However, I soon got back to the routine of the farming calendar and re-acquainting myself with so many old friends and relations. But my thoughts were always with those friends who I had left behind in Rhodesia, and inevitably I maintained correspondence on a regular basis, particularly with the Wyrley Birch family whose letters I always looked forward to. It wasn't easy sometimes to decipher Hilary Wyrley Birch's handwriting which always somehow went around the sides of her airmail letter, sometimes continuing on the back as well, covering the section designated for the sender's address!

Rhodesian politics were often a main topic, especially towards the mid-1960s. By that time there had been a serious deterioration in that country's fortunes after Harold Macmillan's famed speech on a visit to the South African parliament. He stated categorically that the 'Wind of Change is blowing through this continent, and whether we like it or not this growth of national consciousness is a political fact'. That word struck a chill through the white settlers of the former British African Colonies, as many Rhodesians by then had to begin to come to terms with the necessary practical solution of power-sharing with the African majority.

One way forward was through the foundation of the 'Capricorn Africa Society' founded by David Stirling of SAS fame, motto 'Who Dares Wins', along with his friend Angus Graham, the 7th Duke of Montrose, who at that time was prominent in Assembly of the Federation of Rhodesia and Nyasaland as M.P. for Hartley Gatooma.

I do remember the occasion when they both honoured us with a visit to Qwaraguzi, staying with the Wyrley Birches, and after a good dinner we all debated well into the African night, the ideals and aims of a multi-racial state comprising of the two Rhodesias as well as Nyasaland. The society's aims and object was to fight against extremism and racial nationalism on both sides of the divide.

But sadly the Capricorn Africa Society didn't find favour with mandarins back in Britain. By then the Colonial Office was totally on a one vote policy so those dreams of a power-sharing multi-racial society based on a franchised voting system were now dead in the water and the Capricorn Africa Society was wound up.

Prior to the breakup of the Federation work had started on the Kariba Dam which had been planned to assist the emerging nations

Southern Rhodesia (Zimbabwe), Northern Rhodesia (Zambia), and Nyasaland (Malawi) providing a generous source of power. The main beneficiary would have been Zambia with the Copper Belt mines and the smelting of the ores.

During the summer of 1976 Hilary and Wyrley honoured us with a visit which I believed to have been their last trip to the UK as they both were getting on in years. Soon afterwards their eldest son Anthony and his wife Susan decided to leave Africa. Such was the time when the Rhodesian Prime Minister Ian Smith declared UDI on 11th November 1965. Never since the American Declaration of Independence has there been such an affront to the United Kingdom. The immediate reaction from the then Labour government led by Harold Wilson was to blockade all trade with Rhodesia. Smith was charged with Treason by Wilson. The Governor Sir Humphrey Gibbs appointed in 1959 had the insidious task of go-between, himself more or less held as a hostage holed up in Government House until 1969.

The initial response of the British government to this long awaited challenge was to put in place sanctions on all trade with Southern Rhodesia, particularly to prevent shipments of oil being delivered through the Portuguese East African Port of Beira (Sofala). The British Navy established a warship to patrol the coast with orders to intercept any potential blockade runners. However, with the long extended border with South Africa, it was easy enough to trade all manner of goods with a sympathetic neighbour. Also, South Africa supplied a number of steam locomotives thus helping the Rhodesian railways to function with plenty of indigenous coal from their own 'Wankie' coalfield.

Exports of Rhodesia's vital cash crop, tobacco, did cause some inconvenience to start with. However, again with the cooperation of South Africa, Rhodesian tobacco was blended with the Republic's and from there found its way onto the world markets.

Soon efforts to reach a compromise through talks began reso-lution, to be followed by a meeting between Ian Smith and Harold Wilson on board the destroyer H.M.S. *Tiger* in the Mediterranean during October 1966 with no satisfactory resolution of the constitutional crisis. However, a further two years later, the two leaders tried again, this time on board H.M.S. *Fearless* off Gibraltar. Again no agreement was reached. Smith refused to abandon UDI and return to the British fold pending amenable settlement to accept a black majority. Meanwhile 'Good old Smithy's little Rhodesia' began to have a strong following in Britain, especially through the media of the Conservative-leaning press. The admiration of a man standing alone leading a small minority white government, defying all attempts to bring him to heel, made him into a sort of folk hero.

Then on the return of a more sympathetic Conservative government under Edward Heath, Smith struck a deal with the then newly appointed Foreign Secretary Alec Douglas Home that would have legalised UDI, in return for a new constitution pushing black rule into the remotest of futures. However, this agreement was massively rejected after the African population was consulted by the Pearce commission. Now independence before majority rule was unassailable; any hope of securing an independent, internationally recognised white Rhodesia had faded into oblivion. For a while life in Rhodesia went on very much as before. The security forces were more than capable of controlling the guerrilla activities. But by the mid 1970s two events sealed the fate of the Smith regime. Firstly, with the total collapse of Portugal's African empire in 1975 Smith was suddenly confronted with a black ruled Mozambique lying on Rhodesia's eastern frontier which immediately offered a safe haven for guerrillas. The war was now unwinnable coupled with the haemorrhage of white Rhodesians leaving the security forces, the equivalent of a battalion of fighting men a month, as they left the country for good.

The intensification of guerrilla activity was dramatically relayed to me in one of Col. Wyrley-Birch's letters describing in detail the night when the terrorists chose to attack Qwaraguzi.

Both Hilary and Wyrley were rudely awakened by small arms fire targeted at themselves and Qwaraguzi. Their immediate reaction was to roll out of bed and lie flat on the floor whilst bullets ricocheted around their bedroom. After a very anxious period feeling at any moment the terrorists would burst into the house, they were conscious of another lot of small arms fire coming from another direction, but not at them. Their immediate assumption was that the security forces had arrived in a very short time after they had pressed their security panic button, but it was not until the following morning when the security forces eventually appeared on the scene. It transpired that two separate groups of terrorists, unknown to each other happened to target Qwaraguzi on the same night!

This dramatic chain of events was told to me by Wyrley in his letter describing the night of the raid. His comment was 'he did not so mind being shot at', having survived two world wars. But it was the indignity of finding his precious Savile Row suits ruined by bullet holes after his wardrobe had been a victim of the attack.

Not so long after that event the Wyrley Birches left Qwaraguzi for good for the relative safety of Narondere. Inevitably the terrorists returned to pillage and burn Qwaraguzi as that property was so close to the frontier of Mozambique from where the terrorists so easily slipped over the border from their now permanent bases.

The last four years of white rule were coupled with a series of desperate measures by Ian Smith and his government to delay the inevitable as a Labour government had now been returned to power in Britain. South Africa, so long an ally, had now embarked on its own drive for detente with its neighbours to the north, and began to distance itself from the regime in Salisbury forcing Smith to realise his only way out now was to open up negotiations with the two internal black leaders, Abel Muzorewa and Ndabaningi Sithole, and even Joshua Nkomo, the Matubele leader, resulting in an internal settlement with Sithole and Muzorewa being signed on 4th March 1978. But it was too little and too late, as by now Nkomo and Robert Mugabe, the Nationalist leader of the Shoko tribe, had between themselves forged the Patriotic Front. Finally, on 1st June 1979 Ian Smith stood down after fifteen years as Prime Minister to be succeeded by Bishop Muzorewa as the new interim Prime Minister of a Government of National Unity. Sanctions were finally lifted just ahead of a planned all party conference at Lancaster House in London, now chaired by Lord Carrington, the new Conservative Secretary of State for Foreign and Commonwealth Affairs.

He persuaded Margaret Thatcher that both Mugabe and Nkomo were terrorists but they had to be part of any lasting settlement. The Lancaster House agreement was duly signed thus ending the guerrilla war and setting in place all party elections on 1st March 1980, the result of which was a landslide victory for Mugabe. So ended one hundred years of white rule, which had now passed into history.

I for one was left with a sense of bitterness and frustration in not being able to have any influence at all on the fate of white Rhodesians, many whom I had met and knew, who had given all their lives to make a success of their careers and businesses in that lovely corner of Africa. In so many cases they were now the third generation of white Rhodesians, son and daughters of those who had made great sacrifices in two world wars, on behalf of Britain. What was to be their fate? Unless they held British passports, they had nowhere to go, let alone being able to move out any capital or possessions, coupled with a debased currency. A great number did manage to resettle in South Africa; also Australia along with New Zealand gave them chances of new start ups.

Those who returned to Britain found it very difficult unless they happened to have immediate family to support them. One or two worthy charities stepped in to help them in their plight, others or the remainder stayed on in hope of finding a place for themselves under the new regime. Ian Smith was one such person with his farming and family interest. Also, to his credit he had a very remarkable war record by joining the 237 Squadron of the Royal Rhodesian Air force then transferring to the 130 Squadron of the RAF, flying Spitfires. Smith proudly wore his old 'Spitfire' tie right to the end of his days.

The true background to Rhodesia was its agriculture with farms passing through several generations who tended the land with due diligence and care with the help of semi-skilled African farm workers. These farmers were soon to suffer greatly when the Mugabe government through an act of resettlement by the so called 'War Vets' driven by extreme nationalistic greed, incompetence and corruption started to seize the European-owned farms. Not only was this having a catastrophic effect on food production but it was also causing a tide of former African farm workers who in desperation moved into Harare to find some form of alternative employment. This in turn created shanty towns within the city which caused some embarrassment to the government who ruthlessly drove out the inhabitants by bulldozing their shacks. These poor unemployed homeless souls had nowhere to turn to. Many sought refuge in neighbouring South Africa once again looking for a livelihood, such was the tragic fate of Southern Rhodesia.

Looking through the rose-tinted spectacles of the youthful enthusiasm of my letters home those fifty five years ago, I saw a life which could not endure. However, those lasting memories of Rhodesia, its people, and the beauty of the countryside with its extraordinary variety of wildlife, made such a lasting impression on me. This little corner called Southern Rhodesia with its small population of only 120,000 white settlers representing only 3 per cent of the total population managed to stop the clock for fifteen years. I do hope that this event will now go down in history – how a small group of settlers managed to hold back a rampant tide of nationalism, only to be swamped by the incoming tide drowning any hope of establishing a multi-racial society within a nation living in harmony with itself. The remnant are now just flotsam and jetsam left stranded on the African beach of history, on which I end my tale.